The Hidden Power of a Mother's Heart

Lessons on Motherhood
from the Life of Mary, the Mother of Jesus

GLENDA MALMIN

CITYCHRISTIAN
PUBLISHING

Portland, Oregon, U.S.A.

The Hidden Power of a Mother's Heart

In protestant circles, Mary has often been an overlooked individual, other than her necessary role in the Christmas story. Yet, Glenda Malmin takes Mary's story with insight and humor and walks us along the path that every mother walks…from expectant mother to grandmother. She challenges us with our need for patience and trust, confronts our fears, and helps us learn how to release our children into their destiny. She is also not afraid to address the "tough stuff" of parenting. She uses examples of mothers in difficult situations and balances those trials of parenthood with the faithfulness of God. This book is a tremendous biblical study of the life of Mary, and a great encouragement to any woman on the journey of motherhood.

— REBECCA BAUER Executive Director
Women's and Family Ministries
The Church On The Way – Van Nuys, California

Abraham Lincoln once said: "I remember my mother's prayers and they have always followed me. They have clung to me all my life." The prayers of a mother influenced one of the great leaders of the world. As mothers we truly are privileged to form and fashion the next generation. Glenda Malmin's outstanding book gives us keys in doing this effectively and with diligence. A 'have to read' for all those who take this season of influence seriously.

— NICOLE CONNER Associate Minister
CityLife Church – Melbourne, Australia

Glenda Malmin does an excellent job of presenting Mary, the mother of Jesus, as a role model and a woman of faith. You will glean valuable lessons from the experiences of Mary and contemporary mothers, in the area of learning to walk by faith and standing on God's promises through all circumstances. This book will inspire mothers to continue leaning on God and not their own understanding, as they raise children in today's uncertain world.

— *CAROL CYMBALA*
  Director of Grammy Award-winning Brooklyn Tabernacle Choir
  The Brooklyn Tabernacle – Brooklyn, New York

Glenda has done it again. In her unique and insightful style she writes on motherhood, of which she is well qualified, with two beautiful grown children. Having a dear friendship with her for over 30 years, I can say that she practices what she humbly preaches.

— *EDIE IVERSON*
  Ministers Fellowship International

Glenda has written a story about Mary, the mother of Jesus, like none I've ever read. Her comparison to other mothers in the Bible, as well as to some modern day mothers, is very powerful. This book will inspire any woman who is entering motherhood and help her to follow in the presence of Jesus Christ to help her through any struggle she may encounter. None of us will ever face what Mary faced, but we know God's grace will help us go through whatever we experience in our lives. I hope that you, the reader, will enjoy this book as I have.

— *EVELYN ROBERTS*
    Oral Roberts University – Tulsa, Oklahoma

AUTHOR'S NOTE: Mrs. Evelyn Roberts graciously prepared this endorsement for the book prior to her passing in May 2005.

Glenda Malmin uses the story of Mary, the mother of Jesus, to paint a panoramic backdrop of the significance and value of a mother's role. She creatively weaves the threads of this ageless biblical narrative with present-day illustrations, demonstrating how Mary's life is relatable and relevant to the joys and struggles of every mother. Mothers, grandmothers, god-mothers, step-mothers and surrogate mothers will all find great encouragement and godly wisdom in the pages of this book.

— *GINI SMITH* Senior Pastor
    The City Church – Seattle, Washington

The Hidden Power of a Mother's Heart

Glenda's skill in retelling the scriptural stories of Mary, the mother of Jesus, blended with the stories of contemporary women and their gripping circumstances, ignites faith for living and parenting to the reader. It teaches us to identify with and find God's strength to face our own unique happenings in life. In this uncertain world, this is a book which will provide certainty. I recommend it to both natural and spiritual mothers.

— *IVERNA TOMPKINS* Founder and Director
  Iverna Tompkins Ministries

Motherhood is such an adventure...often times overwhelming! Glenda Malmin, in her new book, offers real encouragement to those of us who are on the parenting journey by presenting Mary, the mother of Jesus, as walking the journey with us. I loved feeling that, in many ways, Mary was a mother trying to walk out this parenting thing just like I am! Her wisdom is timeless. There is something powerful about knowing that you are not alone...that other mothers have faced the same situations you find yourself in. Thank you Glenda for writing this very real, very powerful book that every mother should have!

— *HOLLY WAGNER*
  Author of GodChicks and When it Pours, He Reigns

Published by City Christian Publishing
9200 NE Fremont, Portland, Oregon 97220

Printed in U.S.A.

City Christian Publishing is a ministry of City Bible Church and is dedicated to serving the local church and its leaders through the production and distribution of quality materials. It is our prayer that these materials, proven in the context of the local church, will equip leaders in exalting the Lord and extending His kingdom.

For a free catalog of additional resources from City Christian Publishing, please call 1-800-777-6057 or visit our web site at www.citychristianpublishing.com.

The Hidden Power of a Mother's Heart

ISBN: 1-59383-025-4

Table of Contents

I would like to dedicate this book to my mother, Trevah Casson. She nurtured me as a child, trained me as a young woman and released me as an adult to the will and purposes of God for my life. Thank you, Mom. I will be forever grateful for your unfaltering love and unselfish devotion.

I would also like to dedicate this book to my daughter, Angela Prosser, and daughter-in-law, Rebecca Malmin. I am continually amazed by both of you as I watch you pour your lives into my beautiful grandchildren. I will be forever proud of you both. May God bless and guide you as you nurture, train and release your amazing children to "do whatever He tells you" (John 2:5). May your "children arise and call [you] blessed." (Prov. 31:28)

Acknowledgements

Firstly, I give honor and thanks to my Lord and Savior, Jesus Christ, for giving me salvation as a precious and personal gift. Thank You for leading and guiding me in my motherhood journey and for being a constant source of strength.

I would like to thank my husband, Ken, for his partnership in parenting, his faithfulness in marriage, and his encouragement in ministry. Thank you for making me feel secure, not only as a wife but also as the mother of our children. My gratefulness for your leadership in the home goes beyond what words can say. My love and devotion to you will continue into eternity.

Genuine acknowledgements and a very sincere thank you to my two children, Ben and Angela. Without the two of you, the richness of my life experience would be greatly lacking. Your lives not only bring honor to your parents but to the Lord Jesus as well. I will be forever grateful for you both. You bring to my heart an overwhelming godly pride. Thank you for the journey and the memories I hold dear. I'm so proud of the spouses and parents you have become. I'm thankful that our adult friendship will continue on into eternity.

I would also like to acknowledge my incredible in-law 'children,' Rebecca and Jason. Because of you both, I now have the blessing of being a grandmother. Thank you. My heart is truly overwhelmed and my cup is overflowing with the goodness of God because of you. Thank you for not only being incredible parents in your own right, but also for welcoming me into your hearts and lives. It is a privilege to be your mother-in-law; I look forward to increasing friendship in the years ahead.

A very special thanks to my constant, faithful prayer partners. Mary Henderson, you are an amazing comrade to me. I am indebted to you for your prayers, support and constant joy. You are my faithful, "first responder." Thank you for making the time to read, emote, and stretch me to "do more." Donna Chesnutt, I honestly do not know where I would be in my walk today without your constant encouragement and faithful prayers. I know the Lord hears and answers your prayers. Thank you. You are both amazing testimonies of faithfulness and Christian partnership. Thank you for your prayers and never-ending encouragement. I pray that this book will honor the time you have invested in it.

Many thanks to two of my colleagues, Lanny Hubbard and Ken Ross, for aiding me in research for some of the 'between-the-lines' issues in this great story of Mary's life. I appreciate you both; it is an honor to serve alongside of you at Portland Bible College.

I would also like to acknowledge the incredible team at City Christian Publishing. I so appreciate how you each care for the details of every manuscript you handle. You are faithful stewards of that which the Lord has given you. A special thanks to Rich Brott, Casey Corrigan, Joel Kaylor, and Jason Prosser for your constant encouragement and watchful eyes. What a team!

Foreword

Our firstborn was a perfect baby. She slept all night at two weeks, she was easy to wean, was very obedient—if you told her "no" once, she never touched an item again and was a very happy baby. "We really knew how to raise children" or so we thought—THEN came our second one!

Everything about him was opposite. He didn't sleep all night until he was a year old, etc., etc. The Lord sure has a sense of humor and knows how to humble you. When you think, "I really know how!" isn't He good to give us some examples to follow.

In this book "The Hidden Power of a Mother's Heart", Glenda Malmim uses the life and actions of Jesus' own mother to show us some of the gracious ways she dealt with her Son. What a responsibility she had in raising that Child! Many lessons are drawn from her life as a mother, which can be a learning tool for each of us.

Mary showed us how to teach a child, bringing her own up in the ways of the Heavenly Father. She shows us how His actions frightened her (when He was not with the group returning to Nazareth), clearly expressing her concern and disappointment with Him. Also, we learn how she kept many things in her heart and pondered them. In contrast, how often we want to tell everything, but that isn't always the way; some things are meant to be our thoughts alone. Mary also faced trials, learning through Jesus' life and death, how to leave those situations in the hands of the Father. These are just some of the lessons taught by our Lord's mother.

It is amazing to me how often we teach by our words or actions and are not really aware how that affects our children. It may be by words of affirmation or criticism, a pat on the back or a slap on the hand, or just a short statement illustrating a point, but these things leave a lasting impression on the child.

I remember such an experience of a lifetime impact by means of my mother's words. I had been at aunt Ollie's house and she was fixing dinner. They were having pork chops, potatoes and I can't remember what else but I do remember they didn't have the ingredients to make gravy. When I went home I said, "Mom, Uncle Ted and aunt Ollie are having potatoes, but they have no gravy. All she said to me was, "The Lord gives the gravy." I knew immediately what she meant. My father was ill and could not work so we were on welfare but Uncle Ted worked on the railroad. In our minds he was rich. My family was always a Christian family and learned to tithe. With our small income I can never remember a time that we didn't have gravy with our potatoes: The lesson here was that the Lord always supplies the extra things that make the meal extra special—in other words He adds the spice of life to those who follow Him.

That has been with me all my life and Jack and I have learned the truth of the old statement, "You can't outgive God." A lesson learned from a faithful mother.

Mothers are so important in the lives of their children. Every word and action must be weighted.

Read on, dear mother. Learn the lessons Mary can teach you in raising your children, and God bless you in this all important, life-shaping role.

The mother of: Rebecca, Jack III, Mark, and Christa
— *ANNA HAYFORD*
Los Angeles, California

Preface

The journey of a mother's heart is unique to each woman, yet each journey also has threads of common experience—paths that feel both familiar and unknown. The journey converges upon moments of utmost hilarity and moments of dread as well. It contains fulfilled dreams and uncharted territories. It has its hidden moments and it's public ones; it is personal and yet has the power to penetrate the heart of the next generation.

The motherhood journey has a beginning but no ending. Once you open yourself to it your life becomes a continuum throughout the life of your child. The realization that you do not give birth to mere human flesh, but rather to an eternal soul, settles into your spirit in an awe-inspiring way.

Motherhood also has changing seasons. There will be days of joy, when you feel like there is no child quite like yours. And there will be days of frustration and exhaustion, when you are sure there is no child quite like yours. Through my own personal experiences as a mother and by observing the lives of other mothers, I have discovered that the seasons, as well as the emotions, of motherhood vary. I've also discovered that whether you are a single mom or a married mom, your journey has dimensions of commonality with all mothers.

These common threads also seem to be intricately interwoven with patterns I see in the life of Mary, the mother of Jesus. As I have studied her life throughout the years, I've been encouraged and refreshed by the challenges she experienced as a mother. She faced unique challenges, with a unique child.

I'd like for us to take a good look at her life throughout the following pages. I do not grant her any higher status than the Bible does, but neither do I feel that her life is less than a very significant example of motherhood. Her motherhood journey was, in fact, one that was challenged on every side. This ancient Mary was a mother much like most of us. She had questions, concerns, opinions and deep challenges. She was also inquisitive, contemplative and wise. I have found her life to be a heroic role model for positive, and very real, mothering.

Parenting is probably the biggest risk you will ever take in this life. Whether motherhood is your preference presently or not, if you are a mother, you have probably come to realize that there is no one who can affect you the way your child can. Whether you have given up your child for adoption or adopted your child into your life, his or her very existence can affect you. Whether you planned your child or did not plan your child, he or she is a part of your personal life journey at the point of conception. Whether you like your children at this time or don't like them, their seasons of life will affect your season of life. The choices you make in your seemingly most hidden seasons will have the greatest impact on your life and on the life of your child.

One of the wisest things a mother can do is to walk this motherhood journey with someone. Look for examples along the way that will help you discover landmarks of wisdom to hold on to in times of storm. Mary's life is just such an example. Together, we will search out the pattern of her life as a mother and allow her example to shine a light on the journey of our own hearts.

I have placed a quoted portion of Scripture related to Mary at the beginning of each chapter. Then, in story form, you will be introduced to her as though she was living her personal journey before your very eyes. There is a measure of poetic license taken as the pondering of her private heart-thoughts and prayers unfold in each chapter, but as her story comes alive, you will find that her experiences hold many keys to help you navigate through your own hidden and public journey of motherhood. At the end of each chapter is a list of related Bible verses that may be used for personal or group Bible study.

The primary focus of this book is not as much on exegetical interpretation as it is on the personal application of principles of truth in the quoted verses. I would like you to apply to your own life the lessons drawn from Mary's biblical personal account, as well as the account of the contemporary mothers mentioned. Let the hidden power of her journey minister to you and encourage you right where you are.

If you are unfamiliar with Scripture, I hope you will glean much from the account of Mary's life. I think you will find this historical mother to be one with whom you can easily identify. Scripture reveals her to have been friendly, compassionate and caring. She was also inquisitive, sometimes a bit bossy, and yet truly humble and wise. You will read about the pinnacles of her mothering experience that left her so joyful she could do nothing short of bursting into song. You will also discover that her journey contained experiences so deep and sorrowful that any mother who has known sorrow will find solace in her life and in her wisdom.

This Mary was a mother much like you or the neighbor next door or the woman sitting near you at your workplace. The waters of her soul ran deep. As the fruit of her womb—her son—brought challenges to her personal journey, He also changed her life forever.

If you are familiar with Scripture, I hope you will take the time to read the account again and be freshly challenged by Mary's example. Resist the temptation to skip over the scriptural text. Read it once again and allow the account of this marvelous Mary to penetrate your life in a deep, significant and encouraging way.

I believe that as we look at the life of this extraordinary woman, we will discover a common bond with her. She had questions, concerns, opinions and deep challenges in her role as a mother. I haven't yet met a contemporary mother who cannot identify with each of these facets.

My greatest desire is that the reading of these pages will encourage you in the journey of your heart, whether you are a mother, a grandmother, or a young woman desiring to be a mother. Enjoy the story, adhere to the principles, and enjoy the journey! Therein, lies the hidden power of a mother's heart.

The Call to Motherhood

THE HIDDEN POWER OF A MOTHER'S HEART

Embracing the Call to Motherhood

In the sixth month, God sent the angel Gabriel to Nazareth, a town in Galilee, to a virgin pledged to be married to a man named Joseph, a descendant of David. The virgin's name was Mary. The angel went to her and said, "Greetings, you who are highly favored! The Lord is with you." Mary was greatly troubled at his words and wondered what kind of greeting this might be. But the angel said to her, "Do not be afraid, Mary, you have found favor with God. You will be with child and give birth to a son, and you are to give him the name Jesus. He will be great and will be called the Son of the Most High. The Lord God will give him the throne of his father David, and he will reign over the house of Jacob forever, his kingdom will never end." — Luke 1:26-33

Donning her amber-colored every-day dress and her midnight blue head covering, she rolled up her sleeping mat and placed it carefully in the corner.[1] She could do this routine in the pre-dawn shadows as well as in the darkness of night, without disturbing a mouse much less her still-sleeping family. Strands of her curly brown hair fell loosely around her face and her large brown eyes were as bright as those of a young doe, full of hope and adventure. She carefully opened the door and closed it as she joyfully began her usual early morning trek up the hillside.

Mary loved to spend time contemplating her future and recommitting her utmost devotion to Jehovah God as the sun came over the horizon each morning. She relished looking over the rolling foothills of Palestine on her favorite hillside just above the village. It was fun for her to let her imagination run throughout the pages of her ancestors' history and prayerfully imagine the future as well. This hillside overlooking the bordering fertile Jezreel valley, was her special place where she recounted the destiny of those who had gone before her while dreaming of the outworking of her own destiny.

If Nazareth had any prominent citizens within its borders, Mary certainly was not one of them. She was just a common girl who lived in a common neighborhood. It hadn't been too long ago that she had stepped out of childhood into the dawn of her womanhood. Just an ordinary girl, even by her own admission, but she was brimming with life and young womanhood.

Pouring out her heart to Jehovah and contemplating His will was her favorite part of the day. She loved to abandon herself to Him in prayer. He was more than a god to her; He was the lover of her soul and her Lord. It was a great mystery to her why more of her friends and family did not seem to enjoy such an intimate time with the Lord God Jehovah. But regardless of the mystery, she personally delighted in her time with Him and practically skipped up the hillside each morning singing as she came to her favorite spot while letting sleepiness roll off of her like an unneeded garment.

Uncharacteristic of the usual calm of most early mornings, this morning there was a gentle breeze that wafted over the hillside. She sat on the ground and pulled her knees closer to her body and then unfolded the covering on her head and wrapped it around her entire body. The breeze was cool, causing her to shiver, but she knew that in just a few more moments the sun would peak over the horizon and warmth would wash over her. She never tired of seeing the sunrise, she almost held her breath in anticipation, it was like Jehovah's kiss of blessing on the day.

With the openness of a cherished daughter who knows her father's delight she opened the conversation. *Here I am again, Lord. I'm here to have our daily chat; it's me, Mary. Thanks for the sunrise, it feels good on my face and soothes my shivering body. You are so faithful. I worship You with all my heart and trust You completely. But now, Lord, I have much to talk about with you today. In just a few moments the hours of the day will begin to descend on me like raindrops in Springtime, and I'll have barely a moment to think. I know I can babble like a brook some days, but really there's just so much to talk about today. Having been officially betrothed to Joseph now, I want to first say, thank You. Wow God, You and my parents did a good job putting this one together! Joseph is so amazing and I am so ordinary! He's such a man of integrity, and so handsome too. I am honored that You would favor me with such a husband. With You and Joseph both filling my heart, how can I not rejoice! I praise You Jehovah Jireh, You are my provider! I stand in awe of You and of Your favor toward me. You are amazing to me. Your ways are wondrous and Your pathway is sure.*

What started out as youthful exuberance and joy in Mary's heart melted into womanly calm and adoration, she felt overwhelmed with God's goodness on this beautiful sunbathed morning. Her gratefulness for God's favor led her to a place of quiet awe rather than youthful chattiness. She bowed both her head and her body to the earth in honor of the God she loved and trusted. As she lifted her head an angel stood before her and said, *Good morning Mary, you who are highly favored!* Mary began to shiver from head to toe, this time from fright not from the cool breeze. Who was this proclaiming that she, such an ordinary girl from an ordinary town, betrothed to an ordinary carpenter, was *highly favored?* Admittedly, Joseph was handsome and a man of integrity, but she was a common girl, and they were only betrothed, not even married yet. What did this proclamation of being "highly favored" mean? Emotions of fear and confusion were colliding within her.

The messenger continued, *Do not be afraid, Mary, you have found favor with God. You have nothing to fear. God has a surprise for you: You will become pregnant and give birth to a son and call his name Jesus. He* will be great, be called 'Son of the Highest.' The Lord God will give him the throne of his father David; He will rule Jacob's house forever—there will never be an end to his kingdom.[2]

Suddenly Mary's inquisitive nature eclipsed her fear and she blurted out, *"But how? I've never slept with a man."*[3] The angel responded, *The Holy Spirit will come upon you, the power of the Most High God will overshadow you, and the Holy One who is to be born will be called the Son of God. You can verify this word by knowing about another miracle birth about to take place. This day Elizabeth your cousin is expecting the birth of a son, even though she is old. Though she was barren, she is now in her sixth month of pregnancy. Mary, you are highly favored of the Lord, you too will be a blessed mother!*

Can you remember the emotions you felt the first time you took the pregnancy test and found you were actually going to be a mother? If you are a mother, let me say to you what Mary was told so many years ago: *You are highly favored!*

Whether you are like Mary—a young woman in her teens, without a husband—or you are married, three decades older and well along in the mothering journey, you are highly favored. Whether you planned to have a child or didn't plan to have one, if you do have a child, you are highly favored.

If you've given your child up for adoption, you also have been highly favored. It is an honor and a privilege just to carry a child within your womb. In a society quick to do away with unborn children, you have honored God by giving life and opportunity to an eternal soul.

If you have adopted a child into your life, you have been highly favored as well. Even though you didn't bond with the child from within your body, your deep heart-bond rings with a message of hope for life and promise throughout the generations.

To hear the call of motherhood is to hear the words of the ancient yet contemporary text of the Bible: "You are highly favored! The Lord is with you." It is the revelation of these words that will keep your feet on solid ground and encourage you when it seems there are no solutions.

These words can open your eyes to the light of hope when darkness surrounds you.

The title of a book for pastors' wives, written by Gail MacDonald, seems so appropriate when it comes to mothers everywhere; that title is *High Call; High Privilege*. In God's eyes, that's what your call to motherhood is, regardless of your perspective or your circumstances. It's a high calling and an amazing privilege.

To hear the call of motherhood is to hear the words … of the Bible: "You are highly favored! The Lord is with you."

In the Jewish culture of Mary's day, marriage came about in three stages. The first stage was engagement, the second stage was betrothal, and the third was marriage.

The Jewish people believed that the decision to marry was too serious to be left to the dictates of the human heart. Hence, parents would often arrange for their children to become engaged to one another with a future marriage in mind. This engagement was official but not legally binding.

The ratification of the engagement came several years later, making it legal. This was known as a betrothal. The girls were generally in their early teens and the boys were eighteen or older. At this point, the girl had a choice about the marriage decision. However, once the betrothal was agreed upon, it was legally binding; in other words, you were legally married but the marriage was not yet physically consummated. There would be a public ceremony under the Huppah canopy where the intention of betrothal was stated and a cup of wine was shared as a sign that the couple was entering a contractual agreement to be married. The groom would either offer a bride-price or deliver a written contract which included the husband's duties to his wife and the sum due her in the event of a divorce or his death. This agreement was so binding that it would take a document of divorce to break the contract. If the vow was broken during this period, it could be punishable with death by stoning. The betrothal period usually lasted one year to allow the bride to prepare her wedding garments and for the groom to prepare a home for his bride.

The third stage was the marriage or 'wedding proper.' At this time, the bride was prepared by being bathed, anointed with perfumes and ointments, and then dressed in her wedding garments. The groom could only go to retrieve his bride when his father gave him permission to go. When he had the father's permission, he would go to the bride's family home and escort her back to his house in an evening wedding procession by torchlight with the accompaniment of song, dance, and music. There would be an official introduction of the bride into the groom's house, where the huppah canopy was set up. The couple would stand under the canopy and seven blessings would be pronounced over them, the marriage contract would be read, and a marriage feast and seven days of celebration would follow. [4]

With this in mind, most Bible scholars agree that Mary was probably about fourteen or fifteen years old at the time the angel came to visit her. She and Joseph had likely already committed to marriage by having the betrothal ceremony and were preparing for the wedding in the months ahead with eager anticipation. Economically speaking, Mary was a lower-class maiden betrothed to an economically lower-class carpenter. She felt great surprise upon hearing the angel's greeting that she was "highly favored." In fact, Luke 1:29 says that she was "greatly troubled at his words." She had a realistic understanding of ranking in her society. Even though she was in the lineage of King David, she was still just a young maiden betrothed to someone who was not wealthy or influential by any means. Carpentry was a good vocation, but not one that brought wealth or prominence.

When the angel went on to tell her the name and person of her son, she grew even more amazed. The angel said He would have the title of deity, "the Son of the Most High," and the title of humanity, saying that he would be of the house of "David." When the angel said His kingdom would "never end," Mary's practical mind took over. Instead of dreaming about the prophetic cosmic greatness of her son and His kingdom, she wanted to know how this was going to happen.

Her question was not one of doubt, as Zechariah's had been six months prior to this. Zechariah had been praying for a child (see Luke 1:13). However when his prayer was answered, he asked for another sign, something other than what the Lord had just provided him with through the angelic visitation. So God gave him another sign, muteness. Although God was still determined to bless Zechariah, this silence was a bit of a rebuke for seeking a further sign. The next time Zechariah was heard from in Scripture, he was speaking words of faith, not asking for more proof.

Mary, on the other hand, had not been praying about having a baby before her wedding. So when she asked her question about how this could be, she did not get a rebuke; she received an explanation. God does not seem to mind an inquisitive posture. In fact, I think God delights in our dialogue and He loves to amaze us with His vision and purpose.

God delights in our dialogue and He loves to amaze us with His vision and purpose.

The messenger who spoke to Mary was Gabriel the angel. His name means "God is my hero." He was the Gabriel whom God had sent to Daniel of the Old Testament to give him understanding when he needed it (see Dan. 8:16,17; 9:22). Isn't God good to send the right kind of messenger to us at the right time?

Gabriel told Mary, "The Holy Spirit will come upon you, and the power of the Most High will overshadow you" (Luke 1:35). This statement would have taken Mary's mind back to Exodus 40:34: "Then the cloud covered the Tent of Meeting, and the glory of the Lord filled the tabernacle." This glory that filled the Tabernacle was the same glory that would overshadow Mary and her child.

To build Mary's faith even more, Gabriel spoke of her cousin Elizabeth's miracle child. Elizabeth was in the midst of a similar circumstance. She was a chosen woman of God who would not only empathize with Mary's dilemma, but also would identify and rejoice with her in it. What joy, what privilege to know a kindred spirit! God gave to Mary the gift of another woman to understand her and relate to her circumstances.

What was it like for you to hear the call to motherhood? Did you have anxious moments or months of waiting for the pronouncement that you were indeed expecting? Was it a time of joyful anticipation? That's how it is for many women.

Then the nausea begins. Oh, how one remembers the nausea! Other mothers tell you that you'll forget the labor pain and the nausea. Don't believe it. When you've raced to the toilet bowl yet one more time, it makes you seriously contemplate the arrogance of Eve and the stupidity of Adam in the garden. It's that nausea that causes you to look at brave, young expectant mothers with grace and mercy as you watch them turn green and run. Oh, yes, the blessings of motherhood far outweigh the nausea and labor pains, but you don't forget.

I can remember taking college courses during my first pregnancy. The classes were down the hall from the school cafeteria. As I entered the building, with the aroma of breakfast still lingering in the air, I would promptly race to the bathroom, lose my breakfast and then go to the class. Halfway through class I would excuse myself and kneel before the toilet once again. And yet once again by the time class was over. It became a daily routine.

Pregnancy provided some of the most memorable parts of my personal journey in life, toilet bowl and all. I prayed for, hoped for and longed for children; pregnancy was part of the experience. Have I forgotten it? Not on your life! Do I warn other young women who have yet to experience the blessings of pregnancy? Usually not. Do I laugh with (*with*, not *at*) those who are pregnant and turning shades of green as they run to the bathroom? Absolutely.

Granted, not every expectant mother's experience with pregnancy is the same as mine. Some sleep through their entire pregnancy (at least their husbands think so). They sleep late in the morning, early in the afternoon and on into the evening. Their pregnancy adventure is like a bear's hibernation pattern in winter.

Some women are seemingly unaffected by the nausea, labor pains or sleeping patterns. It's the baby in the rib-section during the last month of pregnancy that brings surprising discomfort. Others skip and sing through the whole experience with nothing more than a slight frontal bump in their anatomy, a gentle rolling movement within, and and a "huh huh huh" exhale just before baby perfect arrives in the world. Those are the women who make the movies we all watch before giving birth.

Regardless of what your experience was or what it may be in the future, why not enjoy every phase of your life to the utmost? When you can look across the table at another friend who is also a mother and simply say, "Remember when…?" and that's all it takes to make you both laugh hilariously, it's sheer delight!

Regardless of the nausea, the swollen ankles or the waddle in your walk, there's nothing you'll experience in life quite like the privilege of a life moving within your womb or snuggling in your warm embrace.

Regardless of the nausea, the swollen ankles or the waddle in your walk, there's nothing you'll experience in life quite like the privilege of a life moving within your womb or snuggling in your warm embrace.

I will never forget the birth of my firstborn. At the mere writing of these words, tears spring to my eyes. When I looked at him for the first time, the feeling of awe, privilege and responsibility overcame me. I realized he was not just a desire, a yearning of my heart, nor an answered prayer; he was an eternal soul. What a daunting thought! He was a soul I was now responsible for, a soul of whom the Lord was requiring me to be a good steward.

I felt overwhelmed with both joy and anxiety—joy for his life and fear of whether I was up to the task of raising him or not. I had a deep awareness of my need for the presence of the Lord to overshadow my child and me as He had Mary so long ago.

These penetrating emotions of utter need and utmost joy visited me again at the birth of my next child. Again I felt overwhelmed, humbled and exhilarated. I was shocked by the profundity of the responsibility with my first child and comforted by it at the birth of my second. The second time around I knew exactly where my strength and wisdom would come from and where it would not come from. There's nothing quite like utter dependence on God.

There's nothing quite like utter dependence on God.

To know that God Himself is placing a gift of stewardship into your hands is both frightening and comforting. It makes you want to run and hide for fear of doing it all wrong. Yet it causes you take comfort in the great trust He has placed in you. Your emotions all too clearly remind you of who you are and who He is; you are the created and He is the creator. He is the One you can depend on, and you are the one who needs Him at every turn.

If you are in the beginning stages of your motherhood, somewhere in between, or beginning your role as a grandmother with a fresh opportunity before you, embrace and internalize the words Gabriel spoke to Mary so long ago. *"Do not be afraid...you have found favor with God....The Holy Spirit will come upon you, and the power of the Most High will overshadow you"* (Luke 1:30,35).

You are Favored by the Lord

GENESIS 39:21: *"But the Lord was with Joseph and showed him mercy, and He gave him favor..."* *(NKJV)*

EXODUS 3:21: *"And I will give this people favor ... and it shall be, when you go, that you shall not go empty-handed."* *(NKJV)*

I SAMUEL 2:26: *"And the child Samuel grew in stature, and in favor both with the Lord and men."* *(NKJV)*

JOB 10:12: *"You have granted me life and favor, and Your care has preserved my spirit."* *(NKJV)*

PSALM 5:12: *"For You, O Lord, will bless the righteous; with favor You will surround him as with a shield."* *(NKJV)*

PSALM 30:5-7: *"For His anger is but for a moment, His favor is for a lifetime; weeping may last for the night, but a shout of joy comes in the morning. Now as for me, I said in my prosperity, I will never be moved. O Lord, by Your favor You have made my mountain to stand strong..."* *(NASB)*

PSALM 89:17-18: *"For You are the glory of their strength, and by Your favor our horn is exalted. For our shield belongs to the Lord, and our king to the Holy One of Israel."* *(NASB)*

PSALM 102:13: *"You will arise and have mercy on Zion; for the time to favor her, yes, the set time, has come."* *(NKJV)*

PSALM 106:4: *"Remember me, O Lord, with the favor You have toward Your people. Oh, visit me with Your salvation."* *(NKJV)*

PSALM 119:58: *"I sought Your favor with all my heart; be gracious to me according to Your word." (NASB)*

PROVERBS 3:3,4: *"Do not let kindness and truth leave you; bind them around your neck, write them on the tablet of your heart. So you will find favor and good repute in the sight of God and man." (NASB)*

PROVERBS 8:35: *"For he who finds me (wisdom) finds life and obtains favor from the Lord." (NASB)*

PROVERBS 11:27: *"He who diligently seeks good seeks favor, but he who seeks evil, evil will come to him." (NASB)*

PROVERBS 12:2: *"A good man will obtain favor from the Lord, but He will condemn a man who devises evil." (NASB)*

PROVERBS 13:15: *"Good understanding produces favor, but the way of the treacherous is hard." (NASB)*

PROVERBS 14:9: *"Fools mock at sin, but among the upright there is favor." (NKJV)*

PROVERBS 14:35: *"The king's favor is toward a wise servant, but his wrath is against him who causes shame." (NKJV)*

PROVERBS 16:15: *"In the light of the king's face is life, and his favor is like a cloud of the latter rain." (NKJV)*

PROVERBS 18:22: *"He who finds a wife finds a good thing, and obtains favor from the Lord." (NKJV)*

PROVERBS 19:12: *"The king's wrath is like the roaring of a lion, but his favor is like dew on the grass." (NKJV)*

PROVERBS 22:1: *"A good name is to be more desired than great wealth, favor is better than silver and gold." (NASB)*

NOTES

1   "Men's mantles were usually yellow or yellow-brown. Women's often were too, but sometimes were red or blue or purple." Howard F. Vos, *Nelson's New Illustrated Bible Manners & Customs*, (Thomas Nelson Publishers, Nashville, Tennessee, 1999), p. 448

2   Adapted from Eugene H. Peterson, *The Message, The Bible in Contemporary Language*, (NavPress, Bringing Truth to Life, Colorado Springs, Colorado 80935, 2002), p. 1848.

3   Ibid.

4   Jewish wedding information adapted from Everett Ferguson, *Backgrounds of Early Christianity, 2nd Edition*, (William B. Eerdmans Publishing Company, Grand Rapids, Michigan 49503, 1993.), p. 68.

Changing the Impossibles into Possibles

The angel [said], "For nothing is impossible with God." "I am the Lord's servant," Mary answered. "May it be to me as you have said." Then the angel left her. — Luke 1:35,37,38

He stood with regal posture before her on the hillside. Even though he was tall, because he stood on the slope just beneath where she was sitting, his penetrating eyes met hers as if to underscore the words he proclaimed. Strangely, though the words that were being spoken sent shock waves through her entire being, Mary's ears could hear the familiar blending of the compassion and delight of Jehovah's voice in his proclamation. It's a strange thing to hear a voice while hearing the heart behind the voice at the same time, but that's what was happening to her. Though the angel spoke the message, she heard the Lord's voice speaking through him. His closing proclamation was *"For with God nothing will be impossible."*[1] It seemed as though those words rang in her ears a hundred times within a split second over and over again.

Finally, the emotions of her heart burst within her, it was as if a great company of witnesses, unseen to the natural eye but discerned by the heart, awaited her response. *"I am the Lord's servant,"* Mary answered.

"May it be to me as you have said."[2] Immediately following her response, the angel departed from her presence. She remained on the hillside alone, and yet not alone. The presence of Jehovah was ever so real. It was as if He was alive in her heart, alive in the breeze that brushed through her long curly hair, and alive in the sunshine that ever-so-gently kissed her cheek. She did not move for a very long time. She sat still in His Presence and did not utter another word. It was as though she was tucking her thoughts away in her heart one thought at a time with wonder and contemplation. She did not move a muscle until she could see children playing in the neighborhood below, and knew that her parents would need for her to return and help with the daily chores.

She rose up and began to slowly walk down the hill as she meditated on what the angel had said to her. *"For nothing is impossible with God."* That's what he said. She thought aloud, *I know from the stories I've heard all of my growing up years that this is true. I believe it in my heart.* Stumbling heedlessly over a bush she mused, *as long as I was sitting it seemed that I could slowly gather and sort through my thoughts, but now I am dizzy with the whirl of thoughts racing through my mind! And yet, mysteriously there is but one thought emboldened at the forefront of my finite mind—the revelation of who I am and who my God is. Has there not always been a joyful anticipation of the future deep within my heart? Have I not always been clear on whom God is and who I am? Have the prophetic words of the coming Messiah not been ringing in my heart since I was but a child? Yes, yes, it's all true!*

She began to whirl around, lifting her head-covering up toward heaven as if to say afresh, *I am the Lord's servant; I surrender all to You great Jehovah, cover me with Your love. I am Your servant! Yes, I am the Lord's servant; not my mother's or Joseph's but the Lord's. Yes Lord, let it be to me as You have said. I trust You, Mighty One, and I anticipate the future with joy. Let it be to me as You have said.*

Can you remember feeling overwhelmed, under-whelmed and every emotion in between at the news that you were expecting? You laughed, you cried, and you jumped up and down. You phoned long distance, short distance, any distance you could; you text-messaged, e-mailed, and shouted aloud in a good old-fashioned way. You felt empowered, over-powered and under-powered all at once as the news of a life forming within you became more and more real.

One minute you were in the doctor's office, feeling exhilarated and secure. The next minute the doctor had disappeared. As you got up from the examination table, all of a sudden it hit you: *I'm going to be a mother! Is it really true?*

In the various stages of motherhood, from pregnancy to the young adult years of your child's life, did anyone ever say to you, "You'll make it; you'll do fine, dear."? Was your response, at least in your head, *Are you kidding, I can't do this! I don't know the first thing about mothering! It's great for you to think that, but you just don't know!*

Did the enemy of your soul ever come and whisper in your ear, "You didn't even like taking care of your siblings; how could you be a mother?" Have you ever felt totally unworthy of receiving that heartfelt Mother's Day card?

The enemy loves to take the generalizations of well-intentioned encouragement or the whispers from his own darkness and cause us to forget that it is the Lord who has called us to motherhood; it is Him we serve. Satan loves to get us focused on status and comparison rather than on our role and God's abilities.

Even if you were an only child, a last-born, or simply never took care of another child even once in your growing-up years, you can still be a good mother. The Lord wants to say to you, as the angel Gabriel said to Mary long ago, "Nothing is impossible with God." Remember, Gabriel was the angel who came to give understanding to Mary, and the message that 'God can do anything' was the understanding God wanted him to leave Mary with. You may have many questions about your skills and abilities as a mother or grandmother, but the message the Lord wants you to hear today is that He will help you, for nothing is impossible for Him.

The message the Lord wants you to hear today is that He will help you, for nothing is impossible for Him.

When the angel Gabriel spoke to Mary, the word "impossible" had never before been recorded in any of the ancient manuscripts of her people. In fact, the word "possible" had not been written until Jesus spoke the word "possible" for the first time in a discussion with His disciples about who could be saved. His response to their question was, "With God all things are possible" (Matt. 19:26).

This message had been woven carefully throughout the fabric of ancient history. From the creation of Adam and Eve to the rebuilding of the walls of Jerusalem in the book of Nehemiah, everyone knew that all things were possible to a people who were willing to believe and follow Jehovah. However, when the angel spoke to Mary, Jehovah had not been heard from for 400 years—not since Malachi's time.

For a messenger such as Gabriel to show up and proclaim in such specific terms that "nothing is impossible with God" must have been quite a thought-provoking revelation. To have an angelic visitation was one thing, but to have him sum up the cornerstone message of history in such a succinct manner must have been earthshaking to young Mary. Not only was his proclamation a summation of God's perspective on history, it was also a personalized message to this humble teen concerning her life and the life of her child.

Mary would need this message engraved on her heart to survive the difficult things in the years to come. Not only would her child be unique, but her personal reputation would be brought into question as well, and her life would be affected forever. Could she do all that the Lord was asking of her? She was a simple young girl with a simple desire to serve the Lord in her generation. She didn't have any extraordinary dreams or desires that went beyond what the will of God was. He would take her simplicity and humility and show the world what He could do with a yielded heart.

God would take her simplicity and humility and show the world what He could do with a yielded heart.

In Luke 1:5,6, we meet Zechariah and Elizabeth. Luke devotes considerable attention to issues of status in this portion of Scripture, characterizing both of them as upright and blameless. He strategically notes their location in the Temple, which is the central point of Jewish focus. Luke also notes that Zechariah had chosen the lot to be the celebrant priest for the week. He had been honored to do the sacred function of burning incense. This was the most solemn part of the day's service in the Temple. It symbolized that God accepted Israel's prayers of repentance. It was considered the highest act of mediation between God and man that a priest could perform on behalf of his fellowman.

From the Temple in Jerusalem, Luke takes us to small-town Nazareth and a young girl betrothed to a common carpenter. Mary's betrothed, Joseph, is a "son of David," but he and Mary are not married yet, so Mary has no current claims on his inherited status. Luke tells us later that Mary is the relative of Elizabeth. This would have given her the status of being in the priestly line. However it doesn't truly give her much status from a Jewish perspective, because Jews considered hereditary purity to be passed down through the male. Mary's insignificance seems to be Luke's primary point in his introduction of her here.

In the Greco-Roman world, and in Judaism, the very status of a slave was determined by the status of its householder. So when Mary responds, "I am the Lord's servant," she is acknowledging that her status comes from her relationship with God rather than from Joseph her betrothed or Elizabeth her cousin. That was a bold deviation from the norm.

From this point in Scripture, we see a noted status reversal. Mary moves from being a lowly handmaiden to one worthy of acknowledgment. Throughout Jewish history, proper greetings always were spoken from the younger and less significant to the older and more significant. Also, the man also was considered to be more significant than the woman and was commonly greeted first. This hierarchy of significance seems to have changed for Mary at this point in the Scripture text.

In Luke 2:5, Luke notes that Joseph went "to register with Mary." In verse 16, Mary's name is mentioned before Joseph's. We also see that Simeon, in verses 33 and 34, "blessed them and said to Mary." Rather than addressing himself to Joseph, the supposed father, Simeon addressed them both and then focused specifically on Mary. In verse 48 of this same chapter, we see Mary speaking for herself rather than waiting for Joseph to take the lead in the conversation.

This is a huge jump for Luke to make when, at the outset of the book, he makes considerable efforts to emphasize the importance of status. This is just one aspect of how we see God fulfilling His words that "nothing is impossible with God." Even social status can be uprooted and turned around when God is involved.

I am not implying here that women are any more significant to God than men are. I am merely stating that Mary exemplifies the importance of each individual deriving his or her status from the Lord and not from others. Mary's revelation of the sovereignty and strength of her God, and her humble posture that allowed Him to do with her and her son what He designed, would carry her through every phase of motherhood. Those two acknowledgments, who God was and who she was, were the hallmarks of her faith.

Mary's revelation of the sovereignty and strength of her God, and her humble posture that allowed Him to do with her and her son what He designed, would carry her through every phase of motherhood.

How about you? Do you know who God is and who you are by comparison? Does your mind grasp the measure of what He can do through you and how limited you are without Him? Do you believe that He can turn the impossibilities in your life into possibilities?

God loves you, and He truly does have an amazing plan for your life. The plan He has for you is not the same one He had for Mary. Nevertheless, it is His plan uniquely crafted for you and your descendants. It will require nothing less of you than it required of Mary, a yielded heart and a belief that if He's called you to a task, He will enable you to accomplish it. He will take that which appears to the human eye as impossible, and turn it into a possibility. As you embrace the creator of the possible, that which seemed impossible will become your amazing reality; therein, lies the hidden power of a mother's heart. It's found only in the embrace between a Creator and His created one – that's where the impossibilities are transformed into possibilities.

As you embrace the creator of the possible, that which seemed impossible will become your amazing reality; therein, lies the hidden power of a mother's heart.

Neither the pathway nor the end result will appear to be what was originally imagined or anticipated. Both, however, will be the glorious outworking of a loving Heavenly Father who watches over every detail of His specific design and plan. Embrace the journey and the creator of it, and watch the impossibilities become possibilities. Watch and see that the Lord is good.

I have a friend who, like Mary, received a similar awareness of God's ability to pour out grace for seeming impossibilities. Her awareness didn't come in the form of an angelic visitation but in the form of a baby boy who was severely handicapped from birth.

My friend was, and still is, a firebrand for the Lord and His purposes. Like Mary, she had no desire short of serving God in her generation. Unlike Mary, she was more than betrothed; she was married. She and her husband had started their journey together with joy and anticipation of all God had planned for them. They were a vibrant young couple excited with life and totally yielded to His purposes. They anticipated the birth of their first child with great joy.

When the baby was born, he was diagnosed as severely retarded and terminally ill. He was totally paralyzed, blind and deaf, and had what doctors termed as a 'failure to grow.' He also had increasing seizures and was only able to eat through a tube in his stomach.

The doctors advised her and her husband to let them medicate him but not feed him. The doctors didn't see the value of his life; they looked at him through the eyes of limited perspective and finite human understanding. They didn't know that he was the firstborn of three brothers yet to come. They didn't know how he would stretch and increase the faith of his parents for the future as well as the present. They didn't know how his very life would be as a golden thread woven into the fabric of the lives of those who would love him and snuggle him close to their hearts.

Basically, the doctors simply didn't realize who his creator really was. His creator was not merely the blending of the chromosomes of his human parents; his creator was the Lord God of heaven and earth. "Who gave man his mouth? Who makes him deaf or mute? Who gave him sight or makes him blind? Is it not I, the Lord" (Exod. 4:11)? They didn't realize who would so carefully watch over this baby, and strengthen his mother day by day as well. "See, I have engraved you on the palms of my hands; your walls are ever before me" (Isa. 49:16).

The doctors predicted a dirge of misery for this mother and death for her son. However, it wasn't a dirge that found melody in her heart. It was a sweet song of faith. Perhaps her son would not be like other boys his age. Perhaps he would not have long life, but he did have life. That's what this mother chose to delight in. She refused to let the predicted pathway of sorrow plague her. Although it met her at turns in the road, she chose the pathway of the "possibles" and handled the "impossibles" as they came along.

As it was with Mary, this young mother experienced God's all-encompassing grace as she yielded to His will each day. She too needed insight and courage from the Father for what lay ahead, just as Mary did. This portion of her journey would also be the hallmark of her faith.

This precious firstborn son died when he was 18 months old. His life was brief, but stirred faith and courage in the hearts of all who drew near to him. He engraved a blessing on his mother's heart and caused showers of grace to saturate her very soul. One of her sustaining Scriptures in this season was 2 Corinthians 12:9: "My grace is sufficient for you, for my power is perfected in weakness."

At the birth and death of this very special firstborn son, my friend's heart was forever woven together with Mary's across the ages. Somewhere in the heavens some divine stirring must have taken place each day as she bowed her knee and beckoned gentle whispers from the Lord. She must have listened closely for the reminder that "nothing is impossible with God" and that His grace would be sufficient for her. Then, just as Mary had done long ago, she humbly acknowledged in her spirit, "I am the Lord's servant. May it be to me as you have said."

This mother's heart was tuned to the impossibles turning into possibles. The doctors recommended that she never have another child. They warned that the risk of having another baby with similar handicaps loomed large on the horizon. This mothering adventure had now become more than a brief trek through an unknown land, it had become the pilgrimage of a brave pioneer willing to forge ahead.

At the writing of this book, my friend has one son in heaven and three vibrant, healthy, growing sons who love Jesus. She and her husband continue to walk in steadfast faith and commitment to the Lord and His purposes.

Parents in this or a similar situation often describe it like a planned journey that goes awry. It's as though you spend months preparing for a trip halfway round the world to a tropical wonderland. You save money to purchase your airfare, and do extensive research about the land you are going to visit. You even exercise in preparation for the trip because you know that when you arrive, there will be some mountains to climb and forest trails to hike. You're not afraid of those treks; they're part of what makes the land unique and inviting. You look forward to the challenge before you.

The day comes when you board the plane. You're prepared with knowledge, dreams and well-marked maps in hand. The flight goes fine and the long-awaited touchdown of the plane on the concourse is exhilarating. But as you step off the plane, a sinking feeling sweeps over your soul. Rather than tropical breezes and lush green forests, snow-capped mountains and blizzard conditions greet you.

Nothing you've thought about or brought with you has prepared you for this location. None of your careful research has prepared you for this land. Maps of hiking trails and the lightweight clothing in your travel bag will do you little good here. Though this land has it's own beauty, it's cold and uninviting, and is simply not your planned destination.

It's interesting to note that after the angel made his proclamation to Mary concerning the 'impossibles' and she affirmed the challenge he presented her with, Scripture simply says, "Then the angel left her." It doesn't say that God left her, but it does say that the messenger who came to impart understanding left her.

Have you ever felt like you've just arrived at an unplanned destination you're totally unprepared for? You finally muster up the courage to ask some reasonably intelligent questions and you can't seem to find a knowledgeable person around to ask. In fact, there doesn't even seem to be a person in sight with a sane or compassionate perspective.

Do you remember what you felt like when you first looked at your child and thought, *I've met my match.* You cried out, "Lord, I am incapable of handling this child another day!"

Was it when you had one too many sleepless nights and your baby was still demanding more food and yet another clean diaper? Was it when your child looked at you mischievously just as he was about to put his little finger in a nearby electrical outlet? Was it when the doctor came and told you that your child had a heart defect? Was it when you had to leave your groceries unchecked in the market and chase your child down yet one more aisle? What did you do with that newly discovered feeling of dismay? In that moment, did you identify with Mary? I can tell you that she could identify with you.

Whether your child is severely handicapped, has an attention deficit disorder, dyslexia, or is simply in an annoying or rebellious phase, there are times when you may need to cling to the proclamation, "Nothing is impossible with God." There will be times in your mothering when you've reached that unplanned destination. Your help will not come through your lineage, your identification with your marriage partner or a parenting class. Though you'll reach out desperately for an explanation, you will discover your answer is in a simple proclamation of faith and a yielded heart to the God who designed the journey.

In Mary, we see that God gave His favor to a person who by all cultural standards measured low in status due to her age, family heritage and gender. She humbly received favor from God, wisely discovered her identity by yielding to His perspective and will for her life and bravely accepted the challenge. He raised her from a position of lowliness by choosing her and equipping her to have a central role in His plan of redemption for the human race.

We, too, must derive our status from our relationship with the Lord. Regardless of what challenges we face, we can stand in the knowledge of who He is, not what we are capable or incapable of. We, too, can yield to His call and rise to the challenge He presents to us.

Regardless of what challenges we face, we can stand in the knowledge of who He is, not what we are capable or incapable of.

After the angelic proclamation, "Nothing is impossible with God," Mary simply said, "All right, Lord. I am your servant. Now fulfill all that You have destined for me and my child."

Whether you feel up to the challenge or not, grasp hold of Gabriel's proclamation that with God nothing is impossible for you, your child and the journey of your heart. Acknowledge that you are the Lord's servant and surrender to the Lord by telling Him, "May it be to me as you have said." And when those who would be capable of bringing understanding to you are far from your side, you will also see that His grace is sufficient for your needs.

Changing Impossibles to Possibles

MATTHEW 19:26: *But Jesus looked at them and said to them, "With men this is impossible, but with God all things are possible." (NKJV)*

MARK 9:23: *Jesus said to him, "If you can believe, all things are possible to him who believes." (NKJV)*

MARK 14:36: *And He said, "Abba Father, all things are possible for You. Take this cup away from Me; nevertheless, not what I will, but what You will." (NKJV)*

MATTHEW 17:20: *So Jesus said to them, "Because of your unbelief; for assuredly, I say to you, if you have faith as a mustard seed, you will say to this mountain, 'Move from here to there,' and it will move; and nothing will be impossible for you." (NKJV)*

LUKE 18:27: *But He said, "The things which are impossible with men are possible with God." (NKJV)*

HEBREW 11:6: *"But without faith it is impossible to please Him, for he who comes to God must believe that He is, and that He is a rewarder of those who diligently seek Him."*

JOB 42:2: *"I know that You can do everything, and that no purpose of Yours can be withheld from You." (NKJV)*

JEREMIAH 32:17-19: *"Ah, Lord God! Behold, You have made the heavens and the earth by Your great power and outstretched arm. There is nothing too hard for You. You show lovingkindness to thousands, and repay the iniquity of the fathers into the bosom of their children after them—the Great, the Mighty God, whose name is the Lord of hosts. You are great in counsel and mighty in work, for your eyes are open to all the ways of the sons of men, to give everyone according to his ways and according to the fruit of his doings." (NKJV)*

N O T E S

1   Luke 1:37 NKJV

2   Luke 1:38 NIV

Section Two

Getting Your Focus Right

THE HIDDEN POWER OF A MOTHER'S HEART

Encouragers Worth Discovering

The Lord is with you. — Luke 1:28

At that time Mary got ready and hurried to a town in the hill country of Judea, where she entered Zechariah's home and greeted Elizabeth. — Luke 1:39,40

This is how the birth of Jesus Christ came about: His mother Mary was pledged to be married to Joseph, but before they came together, she was found to be with child through the Holy Spirit. Because Joseph her husband was a righteous man and did not want to expose her to public disgrace, he had in mind to divorce her quietly. But after he had considered this, an angel of the Lord appeared to him in a dream and said, "Joseph son of David, do not be afraid to take Mary home as your wife because what is conceived in her is from the Holy Spirit. She will give birth to a son, and you are to give him the name Jesus, because he will save his people from their sins." All this took place to fulfill what the Lord had said through the prophet: "The virgin will be with child and will give birth to a son, and they will call him Immanuel" – which means, "God with us." When Joseph woke up, he did what the angel of the Lord had commanded him and took Mary home as his wife. But he had no union with her until she gave birth to a son. And he gave him the name Jesus. — Matthew 1:18-25

Mary's mind raced as she bent over the spinning shuttle. She watched as the threads wove in and out smoothly, but her mind raggedly darted from one unfinished phrase of her early morning encounter to another.[1] *"'Let it be to me as You have said.' Did I say that? What was I thinking?! And why did Gabriel leave so abruptly? Could this have been real? Granted, I can be imaginative, but I'm not normally given to such figments!"* She reached for her falling head covering and pulled it back on top of her head without missing a beat at the shuttle. Her mother passed by and gave her a look of approval as she went outdoors toward the fire pit where water was boiling for the laundry yet to be done. On one hand Mary felt excited; on the other she felt desperate. She needed confirmation and perspective. She needed people that were designated by God to give her confirmation and perspective. *Where were the others who would walk this hidden, and yet frightfully public, journey with her?*

Her foot slipped from the pedal of the spinning shuttle and the wheel stopped abruptly. *Okay, heart calm down. Just think about what he said. "Don't be afraid…you are favored by God…" That sounds good. "Your son will be great…" That sounds good. "The Holy Spirit will come on you…" That sounds good too. "Elizabeth is going to have a child…nothing is impossible…" Aha! That's it!* Her thoughts raced even more quickly, *Elizabeth…she's my confirmation! If God has favored her with a miracle, maybe that really was Gabriel with God's message, and not just a figment of my imagination. Maybe it's true that nothing is impossible. Yes, I believe it is. O God, do let it be to me and mine as You desire. I do want to do Your bidding.* Before she realized it, the words exploded from her thoughts to her mouth and she exclaimed, *"I need to go see Elizabeth!"*

Startled at her verbal outburst, her mother looked through the open doorway and asked *"What are you saying?"* Mary quickly responded, *"I must go to cousin Elizabeth's to visit her, Mama. When I was in prayer this morning thoughts of her came to my mind and I felt that I should go and see her before I marry. I feel urgent about it Mama; please say yes."* Having been young and betrothed once herself, her mother was very familiar with the illogical ways of the emotions of a young bride. She smiled and said that she knew of a caravan of travelers going towards the hill country of Judea that she could likely travel with early the next morning, and that she would ask her father for her that evening. She told her to get back to her spinning and trust that her father would have the appropriate wisdom.

The next morning, with her parents' approval, Mary packed and traveled with the caravan to the hill country of Judea to find Elizabeth and the confirmation that Gabriel had encouraged her to seek out. She was both excited and nervous. *If Elizabeth was great with child and the angel's confirmation proved out, what next? It would mean that she was going to have a child, the Messiah child. How could she ever explain that to Joseph* she wondered. *What will this do to him, to his reputation? What would it do to their relationship?* There were so many unanswered questions that resisted the calm that she persistently required of them. But as she persisted over and over again from deep within, slowly they were held at bay. The more she walked and pondered the ways of the Lord, the more deep in thought and barely aware of the caravan of travelers around her she became. Day after day they traveled and day after day her meditations adhered to her heart. The more she pondered on all that Gabriel told her, the more she could feel the Lord's comfort and courage enter her spirit. She couldn't explain it, but in the midst of the wonder of it all she just knew that everything would be all right.

Can you remember moments in your mothering journey when you felt alone and desperately needed other people in your life? Did you ever attend a women's conference on parenting and feel like you were the only one in the room who was sinking lower and lower in your chair as the speaker gave a discourse on proper parenting?

Remember all the speakers, doctors, and child psychologists who told you that if you did certain things you would get certain results with your children? Do you remember attempting to do all those things down to the letter and getting results that didn't look anything like what they described?

As a young mother, I can remember sitting in a conference and listening intently to the speaker talk about parenting. She was inspiring and articulate. It seemed that everything she said, I was doing. I felt affirmed and encouraged. As she spoke, I reflected that my toddler was active and busy but definitely responsive to my intuitive parenting skills. Although I knew I was not perfect, I was feeling pretty good about myself after hearing her speak. You know that 'pride comes before a fall,' right?

Not long after the teaching session, the speaker sought me out. She began to apologize for using me as an unnamed negative illustration in her session on how a toddler can wrap a parent around their finger with their cuteness—cuteness that would eventually turn into rebellion. I was stunned! My mind immediately raced through her message, but I could not see myself in any of her negative illustrations of how NOT to parent. Nevertheless, there she was, admitting that one of the primary illustrations of how NOT to parent most definitely was me. She admitted that her assessment was based on only one observation of me and my child during one particular church service. But it was still an observation that she had shouted from the rooftops, so to speak.

The only reason she came to me was because I had attended the session and she was sure I was offended by her use of me as an example. She was mistaken; I hadn't been offended because I hadn't recognized myself in any of her illustrations, but now I was offended. I felt shock, dismay and embarrassment. After all, I had been feeling pretty good about my child and myself. I was delighted about our potential as a mother-child team (in fact, I still love teaming up with my now adult children in ministry adventures).

Neither my mother nor my mother-in-law was geographically close at hand to give me advice on this part of my parenting journey. However, I sincerely thought I was doing okay. Now, to realize that someone I respected had a word of impending disaster for me rather than encouragement was frightening. I suddenly felt very alone in my mothering journey. I felt desperate for a mentor who would encourage me rather than judge me. I soon began to seek out some women to give me perspective and hope. I was open to adjustments and advice, but what I needed most was wisdom blanketed in hope not predictions of impending doom.

We all need others to come alongside us from time to time. We need those who will encourage us in our motherhood, regardless of the season we're in. We need others who will hear and speak the Word of God to us in truth and in kindness.

Today, I can honestly say that although I was not a perfect mother, somehow in God's amazing grace my children turned out to be incredible adults. Today their children now have me wrapped around their little fingers. The fact is, that most firstborns probably receive more discipline than necessary, the middle-borns really are overlooked more than they should be, and the babies of the family probably get away with more than they deserve. However, all children need discipline, consistency, and overwhelming amounts of love and adoring glances, regardless of what onlookers think or say.

We need others who will hear and speak the Word of God to us in truth and in kindness.

If you've received harsh or alarming predictions about your parenting early in your journey, don't close yourself off. Whatever you do, stay open to the perspectives and input of others. Don't miss discovering the sensitive encouragers while you're attempting to dodge the insensitive ones. As Titus says, let the older women "train the younger women to love their husbands and children" (Titus 2:4). From the outset of your motherhood journey, surround yourself with encouragers.

The Lord's voice was the first voice that came to Mary through His messenger. Gabriel told her, "The Lord is with you" (Luke 1:28). This is a key insight for all mothers. I can only imagine that among the many things that Mary tucked away in her heart, this one was at the top of her list.

The Lord is with you.

It wasn't only Joseph or Elizabeth who would be there to encourage her. It wasn't just the neighbors she had grown up with or her husband's future clientele. It wasn't even the local rabbi or her own extended family that would guide her on a daily basis; *it was the Lord.*

Mary must have meditated on what Solomon had written so long ago: "He who fears the Lord has a secure fortress, and for his children it will be a refuge" (Prov. 14:26). How comforting that revelation must have been. The God she loved was with her and would always be a refuge for her.

And so it is with contemporary mothers. No one can be with you and your children every waking moment except the Lord. The prophet Isaiah promises, "He gently leads those that have young" (Isa. 40:11). The psalmist also promises, "He will not let your foot slip—he who watches over you will not slumber nor sleep. The Lord watches over you—the Lord is your shade at your right hand; the sun will not harm you by day, nor the moon by night. The Lord will keep you from all harm—he will watch over your life; the Lord will watch over your coming and going both now and forevermore (Ps. 121:3-8). Isn't it amazing to realize that the God of the universe is always watching over you and your child?

Isn't it amazing to realize that the God of the universe is always watching over you and your child?

When I look at Elizabeth, I see a godly warm kindred spirit who was just what young Mary needed. Elizabeth was wise and full of grace. She was rich in heritage, a descendant of Aaron and married to Zechariah, a priest who was also a descendant of Aaron.

A son born to Zechariah and Elizabeth would have been automatically entitled to a place of employment among the priests. The double lineage represented huge blessings and priestly rights to their offspring. It also afforded them great respect in the community as a married couple.

However, because the Jewish priesthood was solely based on family descent, and Elizabeth was barren, their marriage was looked upon with sorrow and grief; and her barrenness was considered a disgrace.

At that time, most Jews concluded that if you were barren, you must have some secret sin that God was judging. Jewish rabbis proclaimed there were seven people who were excommunicated from God. The list began with "a Jew who has no wife, or a Jew who has a wife and who has no child." Barrenness was even considered grounds for divorce.

But to God, barrenness was not considered a reproach. Although children are a blessing from God, they are not necessarily a sign of His supernatural blessing. God loves each individual, whether that person is single or married, childless or with a "quiver full" (Ps. 127:5).

God loves each individual, whether that person is single or married, childless or with a "quiver full."

Elizabeth and Zechariah had not known or understood God's reasons for their childlessness, but they trusted in His sovereignty. They hadn't known they were waiting to be the parents of the forerunner of the promised Christ. They hadn't known how detailed God's timing was in their lives and in the life of their child. All they knew was that they trusted God. He would be on time with the answer, and He would bless them and their seed beyond that which they could imagine in their present circumstances. So they waited and trusted.

Elizabeth had known the effect of being in the priestly line for better and for worse. She had known pride and joy in her marriage to Zechariah and she had known shame and rejection in her barrenness. Perhaps part of the reason for the timing in Elizabeth's motherhood journey was to allow her to be a mentor to the young expectant mother who would one day be on her doorstep. She, who was familiar with shame and rejection, would know how to infuse her young disciple with faith for the future and joy in the present.

It was a new day, and Elizabeth, like Mary, had experienced a miracle. She, too, had a special child within her womb. She had learned how to ride disappointment in a direction toward the Lord rather than away from Him, and He had blessed her. Together, she and Zechariah had contended in prayer for a child. They never abandoned their faith in God. They held strongly to the belief that the impossibles could become possibles.

She had learned how to ride disappointment in a direction toward the Lord rather than away from Him, and He had blessed her.

The only way for Mary to check out the angel's word to her was to check on Elizabeth. This was not unbelief but wisdom. She needed someone other than her own ears and perceptions to affirm God's word to her. God had given her the hint; why not move on it? It was the same principle Paul would later teach in 1 Thessalonians 5:21: "Test everything. Hold on to the good."

The day came when Mary arrived from Nazareth to the hill country of Judea. It was common for the door of Jewish homes to be open during the day, and guests would step inside and express a greeting to the householder who would then respond.

In Luke 1:40 we see that Mary entered the house and called out a greeting to Elizabeth. The next verse notes that as soon as Elizabeth heard the greeting, the baby leaped within her womb and she was filled with the Holy Spirit. In a loud voice she began prophesying to Mary about her blessing.

Not only is this a confirmation to Mary, but it is a prophetic fulfillment to Elizabeth as well. The angel of the Lord who appeared to Zechariah in the Temple told him that John would "be filled with the Holy Spirit, while yet in his mother's womb" (Luke 1:15, NASB).

God will place Elizabeths in your life for your encouragement. To find them you may have to make a long-distance call, volunteer to help at an event where other mothers are, or talk with the grandmother next door. These women may or may not be genetically related to you. They may be young or old and they may come in all shapes and sizes.

You'll need them from time to time, and in some seasons you'll need them every day. Often, they will show up when you least expect them, in unplanned places. Look and listen for encouragers; they're often just an arm's reach away.

Is it possible to balance our busy contemporary lives with our mothering? Is it possible to give love and service with abandon to both the harvest field and our own children? When questions like these assail you, that's when you need an Elizabeth to step into your life.

Though still in her twenties, Sharon and her husband, Bob, were veterans to the mission field. She had grown up in Africa, and she and her husband had ministered there a few years together. Now they were in Taiwan, a land new to both of them. This assignment presented Sharon with new and unique challenges. Not only did she need to balance marriage and ministry responsibilities, but she also had to learn a new language. Between being a mother of two active children, ages six and four, learning a new language and ministering effectively in teaching and administration, she was busy needless to say, but she was also incredibly fulfilled.

She loved her husband, her children and her calling; the combination of marriage, motherhood, and ministry suited her well. Her heart was joined not only to the African people and those of her homeland but now also to the Taiwanese people. She delighted in these challenges. However, by her own admission, she sometimes was frustrated by her tendencies toward perfectionism.

Because of her administrative gifts, Sharon loved for things to run according to plan. Usually this was a blessing, but sometimes this asset could become a hindrance and rob her of discovering the joy in the beauty of the spontaneous moment. Unplanned circumstances could shift her focus from people to frustrated plans. If there's one thing every successful missionary knows, it is that even the best-made plans do not always go according to design. Every mother needs to realize this as well. The administration of plans is a blessing but not quintessential for joy and fruitfulness.

Jesus came to die for people, not for schedules and ideal situations. In fact, there is no recorded time when Jesus actually prayed for plans and schedules, but He often prayed for people.

When the time came that Sharon's in-laws were coming for a visit, she looked forward to it expectantly and wanted everything to go well. She was especially excited that they would be there to celebrate her son's sixth birthday. She had planned a special party for his friends and him.

While Sharon was busy with the details of the party, she noticed her mother-in-law playing games with the children and singing songs with them. That day her mother-in-law's actions demonstrated the message: *Enjoy your kids*. Sharon felt a surge of gratitude for this example.

One day during her in-laws' visit, they all went to Sun Moon Lake. This was a special place of beauty in Taiwan. They had previously arranged for a boat ride on the lake and Sharon prepared a beautiful picnic lunch. The planned details for the day were set to be picturesque and memorable.

As they approached Sun Moon Lake, it began to rain; in fact it began to pour. Determined to fulfill the plan of the day, they boarded the boat for a ride on the lake and were literally drenched by the rainfall. Sharon felt both deprived and denied of the perfect day she had worked so hard to plan. She felt robbed of a blessing and developed an attitude to reflect it.

In spite of it all, they found a place near the lake with a small roof over it. With a cloud in her heart as well as over her head, this disheartened young mother began to organize the picnic lunch. Suddenly her mother-in-law jumped up from the table and challenged the six-year-old to run and catch her. They ran and ran until everyone joined in the fun, including Sharon. Once again she had received a penetrating mentoring moment, not from her mother-in-law's words but from her example. This time the message was: *Make the best of life regardless of the circumstances.*

Make the best of life regardless of the circumstances.

A Danish proverb says: "Whoever takes the child by the hand, takes the mother by the heart." [2] The message of Sharon's Elizabeth, spoken not in words but in gracious deeds, engraved a memory in Sharon's heart for the years to come.

It was at Sun Moon Lake in Taiwan, that rain-drenched day, that the hearts of those two women were woven together with Elizabeth's and Mary's of so many generations ago. Together they rejoiced in the knowledge of the joy of life and the laughter of children. Today, Sharon is in her own Elizabeth phase of life and is attempting to impart these same truths to her young Marys. She is now the Elizabeth who plays with her grandchildren and creates an atmosphere of fun for the family that surrounds her.

If you are in your Mary phase, be openhearted to the Elizabeths in your life as they pass your way. Watch for them. When you least expect it, they will be there. If you are in your Elizabeth phase, remember that actions often speak louder than words. Let your heart message be constant and kind in its mentoring. There are Marys everywhere who are watching and praying for an Elizabeth such as you.

Scripture doesn't indicate exactly how long Mary stayed with Elizabeth. Some estimate that she may have remained until the time of John's birth. That would have been approximately three months. We don't know if there was any obvious change in Mary's appearance when she returned home. However, we do have some indication this is possibly true.

Matthew 1:18 says, "she was *found* to be with child." Some scholars interpret this as meaning she was noticeably pregnant. They deem that the original language of this passage indicates that she looked as though she had a "ball in her stomach."

Mary's cousin Elizabeth had been so accepting and encouraging. In fact, she had told Mary about her condition before Mary could even tell her about it. But now, what about Joseph; what would he think of this "ball in her stomach?"

In Mary's culture, if Joseph had decided to openly expose her pregnancy, she could have been stoned to death. At the very least, he had the right to divorce her. Again, Mary had to let God do the talking. Joseph needed to hear from God himself, even though he was a righteous man who didn't want to humiliate Mary or separate himself from her.

Like Mary, we also must allow God to speak to the significant people in our lives. It's not always easy for others to accept our decisions or to accept our children. Even though others may be very close to you, they do not see your child in the way you do. They, too, need to receive an enabling grace from the Lord if they are going to be effectively and significantly involved in your child's life. In practical terms, this means that you may need to give them some emotional space to sort the issues out before the Lord.

In Matthew 1:20, when it says that Joseph "considered this," it means that he was turning the matter over in his mind. As he thought about it over and over, he fell asleep and began to dream.

The angel appeared and spoke to him. He simply told Joseph not to be afraid to take Mary as his wife. Then he gave Joseph the details of the prophetic fulfillment surrounding these events.

I love how Joseph responded. Scripture simply says, "He did what the angel of the Lord had commanded him" (Matt. 1:24). When God spoke, Joseph obeyed. He was a man of simple faith and obedience. Through that response, God would make him the most privileged stepfather ever to walk the earth.

We have no record that Joseph ever did anything short of honoring Mary. He led his family in every appropriate way possible. I wonder if he always, or if he ever, felt adequate to do the job set before him. God had given him this beautiful wife and son to love and to cherish. How would he go about it? No one had trained him how to raise the Son of God, yet this is what was being asked of him. How would he do it? He would probably do it much like you or I would—one day at a time.

I have a wonderful brother-in-law, Tim, who is much like Joseph. He, too, is partnering with his wife in raising some very beautiful children. He's doing his best to impart what he loves to his children. For Joseph it was carpentry. For this young father, at this juncture in his parenting, it's a love for the great outdoors.

One day Tim took his two-year-old son, Jesse, for his first fishing trip. The plan was to take him to a pond that was specially stocked with fish for children to easily catch. When they arrived, much to Tim's dismay, the pond was not open for business yet. So he took little Jesse to a nearby place to fish. He did this without really having much hope of catching anything.

My brother-in-law got pint-sized Jesse all set with his pole and bait and put his line in the water. He started to walk back to the car for more supplies when Jesse began to yell, "Daddy! Daddy! Fishy! Fishy!" Tim turned and could see Jesse's line bobbing in the water. He yelled for him to let go of the pole as it pulled him closer to the water; but Jesse continued to yell. "Daddy! Fishy! Fishy!" Tim got there in time to help the little guy pull a 17-inch fish out of the water. He had to literally pry Jesse's little fingers off the pole after they got the fish in.

The story goes on. A local game warden came by and suspiciously eyed the fish (it was legal for children under 12 to fish without a license, but not adults). He asked Tim if he had a license and was told 'no.' The warden then said, "You don't expect me to believe this little guy caught that fish, do you?" Tim assured him that Jesse had indeed caught the fish. The warden indulgently told him to be careful and assured him that another game warden might not be so tolerant.

As the game warden was walking up the hill to leave, little Jesse put his line back in the water and it immediately began to bob. He once again yelled, "Daddy! Daddy! Fishy! Fishy!" The game warden turned around to see him pull in a 16-incher. The game warden said, "If I hadn't seen it myself, I wouldn't have believed it!" Jesse caught two more fish that day!

I wonder if that's how people felt about Joseph's boy, Jesus. I wonder if his integrity was ever questioned in Nazareth because of the kind of fishing stories that went around about Jesus.

Yes, Joseph was definitely an important "other" for Mary. His integrity, spiritual intuitiveness, and humility were all keys to the success of her personal journey. His willingness to grasp the vision himself was significant. His willingness to be obedient must have meant so much to this brave young mother. Together they would go many places with this unique child.

We all need help from time to time in our mothering journey. Be wise like Mary and seek out the kind of people who can give you strength.

First and foremost, remember that "the Lord is with you" (Luke 1:28).

Next, find an Elizabeth. Find someone who can identify with you in your journey. She may be old or young, but she must be true and full of faith. Find a woman who is humble, full of integrity, and will speak faith and encouragement to the very depths of your soul. When you're down, let her do her job and tell you, "Blessed are you among women, and blessed is the child you bear" (Luke 1:42)!

To those of you who are married, look for the Joseph in your husband. Honor him in his calling and vocation, and appreciate his genuine efforts to provide for you and the family. Whether he is a Christian or not, most husbands respond to wives who genuinely appreciate their efforts to make wise decisions and provide for the family.

Finally, if you are not married, discover your Joseph. Find a man who will pray for you and with you. Find a man who will listen to you and hear from God himself. Find a man who is faithful and will not leave you or degrade you in times of trouble. Look for a man who is spiritually alert and quick to obey God. When all is said and done, make sure he is a man who will "take you home as his wife" (Matt.1:24).

The Blessings of 'One Another'

JOHN 13:34: *"A new commandment I give to you that you love one another, even as I have loved you, that you also love another."*

I THESSALONIANS 4:18: *"Therefore comfort one another." (NASB)*

HEBREWS 10:24: *"And let us consider how to stimulate one another to love and good deeds." (NASB)*

HEBREWS 3:13: *"But encourage one another day after day." (NASB)*

ROMANS 14:19: *"So then we pursue the things which make for peace and the building up of one another." (NASB)*

ROMANS 15:14: *"…admonish one another." (NASB)*

I PETER 4:10: *"…serving one another as good stewards of the manifold grace of God." (NASB)*

COLOSSIANS 3:13: *"Bearing with one another and forgiving each other, whoever has a complaint against anyone; just as the Lord forgave you, so also should you." (NASB)*

EPHESIANS 5:21: *"And be subject to one another in the fear of Christ." (NASB)*

EPHESIANS 4:32: *"Be kind to one another, tender-hearted, forgiving each other, just as God in Christ also has forgiven you." (NASB)*

COLOSSIANS 3:16: *"Let the word of Christ richly dwell within you, with all wisdom teaching and admonishing one another with psalms and hymns and spiritual songs, singing with thankfulness in your hearts to God." (NASB)*

ROMANS 12:10: *"Be devoted to one another in brotherly love; give preference to one another in honor." (NASB)*

JAMES 5:16: *"Therefore, confess your sins to one another, and pray for one another so that you may be healed. The effective prayer of a righteous man can accomplish much. " (NASB)*

I PETER 4:8,9: *"Above all, keep fervent in your love for one another, because love covers a multitude of sins. Be hospitable to one another without complaint." (NASB)*

GALATIANS 6:2: *"Bear one another's burdens, and thereby fulfill the law of Christ." (NASB)*

NOTES

1   "Professionals probably did the dyeing (of fabrics), but housewives did most of the spinning and weaving."   Howard F. Vox, *Nelson's New Illustrated Bible Manners & Customs,* (Thomas Nelson Publishers, Nashville, Tennessee, 1999), p. 448.

2   *A Mother Is to Cherish* (Nashville: Thomas Nelson Publishers, 1994), n.p.

Staying Focused on God's Goodness

When Elizabeth heard Mary's greeting, the baby leaped in her womb, and Elizabeth was filled with the Holy Spirit. In a loud voice she exclaimed: "Blessed are you among women, and blessed is the child you will bear! But why am I so favored, that the mother of my Lord should come to me? As soon as the sound of your greeting reached my ears, the baby in my womb leaped for joy. Blessed is she who has believed that what the Lord has said to her will be accomplished!" And Mary said: "My soul glorifies the Lord and my spirit rejoices in God my Savior, for he has been mindful of the humble state of his servant. From now on all generations will call me blessed, for the Mighty One has done great things for me—holy is his name. His mercy extends to those who fear him, from generation to generation. He has performed mighty deeds with his arm; he has scattered those who are proud in their inmost thoughts. He has brought down rulers from their thrones but has lifted up the humble. He has filled the hungry with good things but has sent the rich away empty. He has helped his servant Israel, remembering to be merciful to Abraham and his descendants forever, even as he said to our fathers." — Luke 1:41-55

There stood Elizabeth, great with child, and glowing with the radiance of the beauty of the Lord. Her pewter gray garment looked as if it could not contain another day's growth of the child that rested within her, and her ankles were swollen from the extra weight that they carried. Her hair looked more beautiful and healthy than Mary could remember from when she had seen her at the last family wedding, even though there were strands of gray framing her beautiful sweet face.

As Elizabeth's two maidens helped her to the bench nearby after her exuberant response to Mary's arrival, they began to raise and lower the great fans that had been on a stand nearby to cool her. Mary stood, still dazed by the words Elizabeth had exclaimed at her greeting. She was amazed that Elizabeth's words were so immediate, seemingly without thought and yet so prophetic. *What is this greeting Elizabeth is proclaiming within my ears?* she wondered. *Her very words bear witness with Gabriel's message. Could this be the confirmation that he spoke of?* Her mind was racing, *I must be walking under a canopy of blessing! I am blessed, my child is blessed and what has been spoken will be accomplished! My heart is overflowing!*

Something began to rise up from deep within her soul. It seemed that the past, present, and future was converging in harmony. Oh, such sweet melody! The depth of her soul responded to the depth of the words Elizabeth uttered. Deep called to deep. Waters of revelation seemed to rush over Mary's soul. Her cup of blessing was full and running over. She had arrived but a few moments ago, and yet it was as if a song created from the past and destined for the future welled-up within her. It was not uncommon for her to sing psalms to the Lord in her early morning devotional time on the hillside, but she certainly was not one to sing out to others. However, as strange as it seemed, she felt that she had to sing what was in her heart or surely she would burst!

Much to her own surprise, in response to Elizabeth's prophetic utterance, an immediate joyful song of proclamation began to pour out of her spirit like a rushing stream in springtime. *"I'm bursting with God-news; I'm dancing the song of my Savior God. God took one good look at me, and look what happened—I'm the most fortunate woman on earth! What God has done for me will never be forgotten, the God whose very name is holy, set apart from all others. His mercy flows in wave after wave on those who are in awe before him. He bared his arm and showed his strength, scattered the bluffing braggarts. He knocked tyrants off their high horses, pulled victims out of the mud. The starving poor sat down to a banquet; the callous rich were left out in the cold. He embraced his chosen child, Israel; he remembered and piled on the mercies, piled them high. It's exactly what he promised, beginning with Abraham and right up to now."* [1]

As the words *"It's exactly what he promised, beginning with Abraham and right up to now"* came from her lips, she fell into Elizabeth's arms, collapsing to the floor at her feet. Both were now weeping in one another's arms with unrestrained tears of joy. Mary could feel the baby leaping within Elizabeth as she embraced her. It was as if there was a divine bonding between the two sons who were still treasures in the darkness of their mothers' wombs. Unknown and hidden miracles took place in those moments that likely could only be seen from heaven's field of vision.

Have you ever felt so overwhelmed with the goodness of God that you could barely contain yourself? Have you ever felt so excited about the potential you saw in your child that you wanted to stand and cheer, "That's my child!" Have you ever felt so proud of your child that you almost felt sorry for every other parent in the room? Have you ever just wanted to shout, "It's me and that's mine—how about that kid!"

Upon reaching her destination and hearing Elizabeth's proclamation, Mary could barely contain herself. She was filled with melody that intertwined her present joy with the harmony of the ages. She could do nothing short of bursting into song as her heart overflowed with exaltation and prophetic revelation. This was indeed a stellar musical, not to be performed on stage, but where the home fires burned brightly.

Mary totally abandoned herself to the Lord and His purposes. She declared her commitment to God and declared her gratitude as well. Then prophetic insight flooded her soul and the song residing within her was released.

Proclamations of God's goodness, justice, and destiny for mankind were spoken in harmony with heaven on that day. They were spoken in a hidden place in the hill country of Judea, and yet they were no less profound to the destiny of mankind than if they had been proclaimed from a platform in the largest amphitheater in Rome or on the steps of the Temple in Jerusalem. It was these words, spoken by the Spirit of God through his humble and willing vessels that were etched on the walls of human history that day.

There was another woman in biblical history that proclaimed a similar message. Her name was Hannah. She was the mother of the prophet Samuel. She, too, had abandoned herself and her son to God's purposes. She, too, had something to herald.

Unlike Mary, Hannah had been married for many years prior to the birth of her son. In desperation for a child, Hannah prayed, "O Lord Almighty, if you will only look upon your servant's misery and remember me, and not forget your servant but give her a son, then I will give him to the Lord for all the days of his life." (1 Sam. 1:11)

The Lord heard and answered Hannah's prayer. He blessed her with a son. After she weaned him, she brought him to the Temple of the Lord as she had promised. In bringing him to the priest, she said, "I prayed for this child, and the Lord has granted me what I asked of him. So now I give him to the Lord. For his whole life he will be given over to the Lord" (1 Sam. 1:27,28).

Upon making this dedication, her heart rejoiced and prophetic insight flooded her soul. In that instant, her soul became intertwined not only with the young Mary of the future but with her Messiah as well.

Hannah's acclamation met with Mary's song across the ages as she proclaimed:

My heart exults in the Lord; my strength is exalted in the Lord. My mouth derides my enemies, because I rejoice in thy salvation. There is none holy like the Lord, there is none besides thee; there is no rock like our God. Talk no more so very proudly, let not

arrogance come from your mouth; for the Lord is a God of knowledge, and by him actions are weighed. The bows of the mighty are broken, but the feeble gird on strength. Those who were full have hired themselves out for bread, but those who were hungry have ceased to hunger. The barren has borne seven, but she who has many children is forlorn. The Lord kills and brings to life; he brings down to Sheol and raises up. The Lord makes poor and makes rich; he brings low, he also exalts. He raises up the poor from the dust; he lifts the needy from the ash heap, to make them sit with princes and inherit a seat of honor. For the pillars of the earth are the Lord's, and on them he has set the world. He will guard the feet of his faithful ones; but the wicked shall be cut off in darkness; for not by might shall a man prevail. The adversaries of the Lord shall be broken to pieces; against them he will thunder in heaven. The Lord will judge the ends of the earth; he will give strength to his king, and exalt the power of his anointed.
(1 Sam. 2:1-10, RSV)

Through their heart responses to God, Mary's and Hannah's affirmations were interlaced as a harmonious duet throughout the ages. Through these two mothers, God networked the old with the new.

Both women had a prayer of gratefulness and prophetic proclamation. Both were enraptured with God's goodness to them and to the generations to come. From both came a resounding, "My spirit has rejoiced in God!"

At this point, both mothers still faced their greatest challenges. Mary still had to face Joseph, Simeon, Anna, and the multitude of people who would send her son to the Cross. Hannah still had to wean her son and give him up to an undiscerning priest who had raised reprobate sons. She also had to face the surprise and confusion of her husband, Elkanah, as well as the continued mockery of Peninnah.

Yes, challenges were still in the forecast, but these two women chose to relish the moment and rejoice in it. This pattern of gratefulness would carry them through the events yet to come.

How long has it been since you have rejoiced in God's goodness? How long has it been since an expression of joy and delight in the Lord has found a way into your heart and out of your mouth?

If you are in a season when children are crawling out of their beds and waking you up before your body has adequately rested, that's all the more reason to take a moment to focus. I'm not suggesting an hour of prayer on your knees, just a simple "Good morning Lord—I'm choosing to rejoice in Your presence today in the midst of my present challenges."

If it has been awhile since you've started your day off with focused gratefulness to the Lord, I encourage you to take a minute to do so. Don't focus on the impossibles; focus on the possibles. If your child is in a difficult season, focus not on his or her weakness but rather on the power of God's grace working in that child.

Whether you approach your day with joy and faith or with sorrow and apprehension will be determined by your early morning focus. That, in and of itself, can influence your child's attitude and perspective on his or her potential.

Whether you can see the blessings of God in your child or not, they are there. Hebrews 11:1,2 says, "Now faith is being sure of what we hope for and certain of what we do not see. This is what the ancients were commended for." It is in focused faith in God's good will for you and your child that you will discover His blessings.

It is in focused faith in God's good will for you and your child that you will discover His blessings.

One brave mother I know learned early in her journey how to focus her faith. Her name is Vickie. She was 19, and her husband, Rod, was 21 when their son Jimmy was born. By medical standards, as well as their own, little Jimmy was perfect in every way. Life was going great for them, and proclamations of faith came easily.

As is typical with many new babies, Jimmy woke up a lot during the night. Although it was tiring for his parents, they didn't mind getting up with him. He was their delight, their firstborn son.

When he was five months and twelve days old, they awakened in the morning and realized they had slept through the night. Rod went to check on Jimmy and discovered he had died in the night. Vickie immediately called the paramedics as Rod attempted to resuscitate their infant son, but there was nothing anyone could do; little Jimmy was gone.

This beautiful young mother cried from deep within, "Why him? And why me?" The joy of motherhood had been ripped from her grasp. Proclamations of faith evaded her thoughts as well as her speech for days and weeks, only to return to her ever-so-gently once again.

Two years later, a second son, Andy, was born. He too was vibrant and healthy. When he was five months and twelve days old, Vickie and Rod slept fitfully by his bedside, watching over every breath he took. After they passed this emotional hurdle, they began to relax and focus their faith on the blessings of the Lord more completely once again. Gratefulness and praise began to emerge afresh in their hearts.

Fifteen months later, a third son came into their lives; his name was Aaron. The morning after Aaron's birth, the doctor came in to see Vickie and told her that Aaron was born with Down's syndrome. Rod arrived at the hospital soon after the doctor's visit, and although this news was a surprise to them, together they asked the Lord, "Why did You *bless* us with this child?" Gratefulness for this new life and new trust reigned in their spirits. There was no downcast "Why us?" in their hearts. They received little Aaron's life with joy as a blessing, just as the Lord intended. Days of question and despondency were far behind them; they were grateful for the children that the Lord had given to them and considered each one as God's good gift to them.

These two amazing parents have made it a pattern in their lives to support and encourage all of their children. They have done their best to instill in their children Christian principles of kindness and consideration toward others. Little Aaron was no exception to their tutelage in this area.

When he was eight years old, he began to compete in athletic events in the Special Olympics for handicapped children. In the fall he played volleyball, in the winter he played basketball, and in the spring he did track events.

When he was 10 years old, he ran in a track event in the Special Olympics state competition. It was his first opportunity to "run for the gold." He was running the 200-meter race and was far ahead of the other children. When he was approximately 15 feet from the finish line, he stopped and waved for the other five children to hurry and run fast. One girl tripped and fell; he went back and helped her up. After all the other participants crossed over the finish line, he crossed over, shouting with joy, "I won! I won!"

This win would have been his very first medal, as well as his first "gold." Instead, he received a sixth-place ribbon from the judges. But he received a gold medal of pride and joy from his parents. He did indeed win. Vickie's maternal buttons were popping that day. Her heart rejoiced in the stamp of God's character on her son's life.

Today, Aaron is a young adult. By the time he was 18 years old, he had won approximately 20 bronze, silver, and gold medals in Special Olympic events of all kinds. Even though he learned how to win a race or an event, that is not his primary claim to fame. Rather, he has always been known as a kind and considerate young man with a heart of gold who brings joy to many in need of a smile or a warm embrace.

You cannot be around Rod and Vickie for very long without joy and gratefulness rubbing off on you. They, like Mary and Hannah, have experienced challenges in their parenting journey, yet time and time again have found themselves standing in wonder at the goodness of God.

Not only has God blessed them now with four vibrant children who are a strong testimony for Christ, but they also have another child who is waiting for them in heaven. Vickie is forever grateful for God's good work in their lives. Truly this beautiful mother's heart proclaims along with Mary and Hannah, "My spirit has rejoiced in God!"

There are three proclamations that both Mary and Hannah declared following their words of gratitude. They heralded the news that God had turned the tables and righted the wrongs. In doing so, they proclaimed that He was bringing death to man's pride, prejudice and greed. They proclaimed that His work in their lives was evidence of these realities, now and in the future. Everything within them shouted, "Look at me; I am evidence of God's great love! I'm just a humble woman, but God is using me and my child!"

Through these proclamations, Mary and Hannah proclaimed God's message of unfathomable love to all humanity. Their pronouncements preceded the coming of the Messiah and made an indelible mark on the generations to come, for He did come and validate their claims.

> For God so loved the world that he gave his one and ony Son that whoever believes in him shall not perish but have eternal life. For God did not send his Son into the world to condemn the world, but to save the world through him. Whoever believes in him is not condemned, but whoever does not believe stands condemned already because he has not believed in the name of God's one and only Son. This is the verdict: Light has come into the world, but men loved darkness instead of light because their deeds were evil. Everyone who does evil hates the light, and will not come into the light for fear that his deeds will be exposed. But whoever lives by the truth comes into the light, so that it may be seen plainly that what he has done has been done through God. (John 3:16-21)

When Jesus' human birth came through a humble maiden, He literally scattered the proud in the imagination of their hearts. He also exalted the lowly and filled the hungry.

Obviously, our children are not the coming Messiah. However, the question must be asked of every mother, 'What faith proclamations have you been making to your children?' Perhaps your children will also have an integral part in bringing death to pride, prejudice and greed. As Christian mothers, we certainly should be modeling and teaching them to do so. What vision do you have for your children, and what are the words your children hear you speak about them?

When I was expecting my firstborn child, I read that the Muslims credited much of their success to the powerful influence of their mothers. I read that it was not uncommon for mothers to repeatedly say to their young children throughout the day, "Jehovah is our God. Mohammed is our prophet."

When I read this I decided to turn this upside down on its head and use it for the Lord. So when my children were babes in my arms, I continually told them, *"Jesus, who is the King of kings and the Lord of lords, loves you and has a special plan for your life."* I repeated this as part of my nightly routine with them when they were growing up as well. As they got older, I changed the words a bit, but the message was always the same.

These were not mere words I spoke out of reaction to another religion. These were words of life I would stake my life on. These words became so familiar to my children that if I ever neglected to say them before I turned out the light at bedtime, they would remind me before I left the room: "Say it, Mommy, 'Jesus loves me and has a special plan for my life.'" I would agree and then we would repeat it together. Today, they are repeating those same words into the ears and hearts of their children, and are quick to remind me to be sure and do so as well when I am the one in attendance at bedtime. The impact of those words made their mark, and I am forever grateful.

A few years ago I received a note from my young adult daughter, who is excited about life and the future the Lord has for her. She wrote, "You wrote scriptures on my heart, and a sense of destiny and purpose. When you said every night 'Jesus has a special plan for your life,' I believed you…and I still do."

"You wrote scriptures on my heart, and a sense of destiny and purpose. When you said every night 'Jesus has a special plan for your life.' I believed you...and I still do."

Just as the bedtime words were etched on the canvas of my daughter's heart, her words of appreciation and acceptance of them have indelibly marked mine. In some inalterable way, my heart rejoices and is interlaced with Mary's and Hannah's forever.

A mother's words are powerful. We must be ever faithful to speak words of reality and faith into the hearts of our children. Proverbs 18:21 says, "The tongue has the power of life and death, and those who love it will eat its fruit." Proverbs 15:4 says, "The tongue that brings healing is a tree of life."

You cannot speak into your child a destiny the Lord has not determined for him or her. However, you can instill faith and belief in them to become all that God has destined them to be.

You cannot speak into your child a destiny the Lord has not determined for him or her. However, you can instill faith and belief in them to become all that God has destined them to be. One unknown poet put it this way:

> I took a piece of plastic clay
> And idly fashioned it one day.
> And as my fingers pressed it still,
> It bent and yielded to my will.
> I came again when days were past,

The bit of clay was hard at last.

My early impress still it bore,

And I could change its form no more.

You take a piece of living clay

And gently form it day by day,

Molding with your power and art,

A young boy's soft and yielding heart.

You come again when years are gone,

It is a man you look upon.

Your early impress still he bore

And you can change him never more.

With all the challenges that come, motherhood is still one of the greatest blessings that will ever cross a woman's pathway. Allow me to paraphrase Matthew 5:3-11 to put these blessings into perspective.

A MOTHER'S BEATITUDES

+ *Blessed is the mother* whose children freely laugh, play and pray, for hers is the kingdom of heaven on earth.

+ *Blessed is the mother* who cries when she needs to but does not lack faith, for she will be comforted.

+ *Blessed is the mother* who has a gentle disposition in the midst of the fluctuating emotions of her children, for she will inherit their hearts.

+ *Blessed is the mother* who hungers for a closer walk with God, for she will be nourished and sustained.

+ *Blessed is the mother* who is merciful in moments of contradiction, for she will receive mercy in the days that lie ahead.

+ *Blessed is the mother* who is pure in heart and in spirit, for she will see God and the future in the eyes of her children.

+ *Blessed is the mother* who is a peacemaker in times of storm, for she will be called trustworthy and true.

+ *Blessed is the mother* who is disheartened in the journey, for there is hope and a future for her.

+ *Blessed is the mother* who alone can see her child's potential, for God Himself will be her rear guard.

> *Blessed mother, rejoice and be glad,*
> *because great is your reward in heaven.*

Motherhood will require more than you have to give, but the blessings will far outweigh the challenges because the grace of the Lord Jesus will be with you (see 1 Cor. 16:23).

Acknowledge along with Elizabeth that you are "blessed…among women." Proclaim with Mary that your "soul glorifies the Lord" and your "spirit rejoices in God." In these proclamations you will find a song in your heart and a grace that will sustain you for the journey ahead.

Focusing on God's Goodness

2 CHRONICLES 6:41: *"Now arise, O Lord God, and come to your resting place, you and the ark of your might. May your priests, O Lord God, be clothed with salvation, may your saints rejoice in your goodness." (NIV)*

PSALMS 21:3: *"For You meet him with the blessings of goodness; You set a crown of pure gold upon his head." (NKJV)*

PSALMS 23:6: *"Surely goodness and mercy shall follow me all the days of my life; and I will dwell in the house of the Lord forever." (NKJV)*

PSALMS 27:13: *"I would have lost heart, unless I had believed that I would see the goodness of the Lord in the land of the living." (NKJV)*

PSALMS 31:19: *"How great is your goodness, which you have stored up for those who fear you, which you bestow in the sight of men on those who take refuge in you." (NIV)*

PSALMS 33:5: *"He loves righteousness and justice; the earth is full of the goodness of the Lord." (NKJV)*

PSALMS 52:1: *"The goodness of God endures continually." (NKJV)*

PSALMS 65:11: *"You crown the year with Your goodness, and Your paths drip with abundance." (NKJV)*

PSALMS 68:10: *"You, O God, provided from Your goodness for the poor." (NKJV)*

PSALMS 107:9: *"For He satisfies the longing soul, and fills the hungry soul with goodness." (NKJV)*

ROMANS 2:4: *"Or do you despise the riches of His goodness, forbearance, and longsuffering, not knowing that the goodness of God leads you to repentance?" (NKJV)*

ROMANS 15:14: *"Now I myself am confident concerning you, my brethren, that you also are full of goodness, filled with all knowledge, able also to admonish one another." (NKJV)*

GALATIANS 5:22,23: *"But the fruit of the Spirit is love, joy, peace, long-suffering, kindness, goodness, faithfulness, gentleness, self-control. Against such there is no law." (NKJV)*

EPHESIANS 5:9: *"For the fruit of the Spirit is in all goodness, righteousness, and truth." (NKJV)*

2 THESSALONIANS 1:11,12: *"Therefore we also pray always for you that our God would count you worthy of this calling, and fulfill all the good pleasure of His goodness and the work of faith with power, that the name of our Lord Jesus Christ may be glorified in you, and you in Him, according to the grace of our God and the Lord Jesus Christ."*

NOTES

1   Eugene H. Peterson, *The Message, The Bible in Contemporary Language,* (NavPress, Bringing Truth to Life, Colorado Springs, Colorado 80935, 2002), p. 1849,1850.

Flowing with God's Timetable

In those days Caesar Augustus issued a decree that a census should be taken of the entire Roman world....And everyone went to his own town to register. So Joseph also went up from the town of Nazareth in Galilee to Judea, to Bethlehem the town of David, because he belonged to the house and line of David. He went there to register with Mary, who was pledged to be married to him and was expecting a child. While they were there, the time came for the baby to be born, and she gave birth to her firstborn, a son....And there were shepherds living out in the fields nearby, keeping watch over their flocks at night. An angel of the Lord appeared to them, and the glory of the Lord shone around them, and they were terrified. But the angel said to them, "Do not be afraid. I bring you good news of great joy that will be for all the people. Today in the town of David a Savior has been born to you; he is Christ the Lord. This will be a sign to you: You will find a baby wrapped in cloths and lying in a manger." So they hurried off and found Mary and Joseph, and the baby, who was lying in the manger. When they had seen him, they spread the word concerning what had been told them about this child, and all who heard it were amazed at what the shepherds said to them. But Mary treasured up all these things and pondered them in her heart. — Luke 2:1-12, 16-19

Once again Mary sat at her spinning wheel contemplating another journey, only this time she was the one who was great with child. It was her tunic that was about to burst at the seams, not Elizabeth's. When she stood it felt fine, but when she sat, it felt tight across her abdomen. Bending over the shuttle was no easy task these days, but she needed to finish this last swaddling band before finishing her packing. She and Joseph were heading to Bethlehem the very next day to register for the census, and her baby would very likely be born before she returned home.

The swaddling bands, Mary had sewn for her soon-coming son, were simple but precious. Most of them were ecru in color, but she had one, that she had woven with an extra layer of thickness and then had it dyed purple for some work that Joseph traded with the man who lived two streets over who dyed cloth as a business. She, herself, did not have a dress or tunic dyed in such a royal color, but she thought it only befitting for her very special child. It was such a small piece of fabric that the trade labor was really only minimal. She planned to use this purple blanket for baby Jesus as an outer covering since it was thicker than the other swaddling cloths. It would keep him warm. The nights were cold now and she did not want her newborn to ever feel the chill of night.

She leaned back and reached for her hot tea and figs and pondered how strange it was to know that she was having a baby boy and that his name would be Jesus. Even simple details like this still amazed her. Of course, to be giving birth to the Son of God was certainly the greater secret. But even just to know his gender and his name before his birth was a unique delight to her. Most expectant mothers could only guess, but she knew. When the old women in the market place wanted to draw her into a guessing match about what gender her firstborn child would be, she would shyly confess that her heart would rejoice with whatever Jehovah saw fit to bless her and Joseph with.

Now more into thought and enjoying her tea and figs, she leaned back against the wall behind her as Joseph passed by the door and caught her eye with a smile. His affirming smile stirred her to thoughts of him and memories of the beauty of the simplicity of their wedding day so many months ago. After Joseph's visitation with the angel, he graciously took the brunt of the family's criticism for wanting to marry sooner than planned. He said that he could not wait for the remaining months to pass for the typical year's betrothal.

Her family was quietly suspicious of Mary's obvious weight-gain after she returned home from Elizabeth's, but they never asked the questions they feared the most.[1] For her to be unfaithful to Joseph would have been impossible for them to believe, and anything else did not make sense. They trusted their beautiful young Mary and knew her as only completely devoted to Jehovah God and His purposes. They knew Joseph to be the same. So when Joseph insisted on marrying sooner than planned, though frustrated initially, they agreed to his request.

Later, when it was their right and duty to request the 'tokens of virginity,' Joseph told them that it would not be necessary.[2] He assured them that he was committed to her for life and that no cruel accusation would ever come from his lips about his beloved. Mary was amazed by the strength of his love for her. His integrity and obvious protection of her was awe-inspiring to all that were within the immediate range of observation. Whether they understood or agreed with his decisions or not, Joseph had the respect of those in the nearby community.

The wedding had been simple, due to the lack of time in planning. There was no torchlight processional, no musical instruments, singers or dancers. Joseph simply arrived at her father's door at a designated time with one other of his friends. Upon seeing her, he placed bracelets upon her wrists, a necklace around her neck, and earrings in her ears.[3] As he adorned her with these precious family heirlooms, his eyes sparkled as did hers. He then escorted her to his home with simple dignity and grace, with her family in tow.

Mary wore a beautiful dress of white linen and embroidered cloth with a long bridal veil trimmed in fresh flowers. She was as beautiful and pure as any bride who had ever come before the presence of a Holy God. She carried herself with a queenly dignity that would make the heart of any king skip a beat and long to protect and provide for her. Though simply adorned, she was radiant to behold.

The huppah canopy was set up behind Joseph's home and carpentry shop and the local synagogue ruler was present to pronounce the seven blessings over them. When Mary and Joseph stepped under the huppah, Joseph lifted her veil and they were both crowned with garlands of rue upon their heads.[4] The evening candlelight under the canopy sparkled around the brown curls that delicately framed Mary's face. Her countenance glowed with love for Joseph.

As the blessings were pronounced Joseph looked adoringly into her beautiful brown eyes as if to say, *I will love you and care for you all the days of my life. I will protect you and provide for you. No matter what comes, I'll be by your side as long as I have breath.* As her inward interpretations of Joseph's obvious adoration lingered reflectively in the pools of his eyes, the marriage contract was read. Following the benediction, the prescribed washing of hands followed and they were pronounced husband and wife.[5]

Next came a delicious roast lamb celebration dinner with the few family members and close friends that were in attendance. Although they did not have the usual seven days of festivities following their wedding, and the wedding was not elaborate in ceremony, it was endearing to the hearts involved. The conversation around the celebration table was joyous; there was a definite awareness of God's holiness, His pleasure and His joy that was felt by all. The Presence of Jehovah was so evident throughout the evening that His blessing could not be denied by anyone present.

As the next two months flew by, it became obvious that Mary was with child, but no one spoke openly with Joseph or her about it. Joseph was so adoringly protective of her that no one dare cross that threshold. Even though they both knew that the neighbors were gossiping about it, no one was openly confrontational. Mary was careful about how often she went to the marketplace in public, but she wasn't in total seclusion.

The love between Mary and Joseph was tender and secure; they held a secret between them that no one else could know or understand. They cherished those first quiet months together. They learned to love and care for one another in a way that most newlyweds do not. Mary loved to serve Joseph and he loved to serve her. Together they prayed for their firstborn son and the grace to raise him in the wisdom and admonition of the Lord. Hardly a day went by that they did not talk about baby Jesus and what it would be like to raise him. They spent more time in prayer together than either of them had imagined they would. Mary shared her favorite morning devotional spot on the hillside with Joseph, and they went there together most mornings.

They learned to read each other's eyes and respond to one another's gentle touches. They laughed together, cried together, prayed together, and worked together. Even though they planned for the future together as well, they always added to every conversation concerning it simultaneously, *"if the Lord wills…"* and then chuckled with knowing delight that Jehovah would have His way.

In the past few weeks, the whispers and critical glances of the neighborhood women seemed to have ceased and Mary was confident they would be there for her at the birth of her son. Nazareth was home; she felt that it was a safe place for her child to be born. She so longed for him to be in a comfortable place when he was born. Knowing that he was a boy, she had so looked forward to hearing the traditional rejoicing of the minstrels and singers at his birth, especially since there had been none at her wedding.

But now that Joseph had to go to Bethlehem for the census and was insisting on her going with him, she was in a bit of a quandary. *Who would give her son an appropriate welcome in Bethlehem, a city full of strangers? Who would sing a song of jubilation for her firstborn son? Could she make the journey?* From Nazareth to Bethlehem it was almost 80 miles; that was at least a four-day journey. *Would she make it, or would her son be born on the roadside?* And yet, she totally trusted Joseph and his judgment. He did not want to leave her alone when she was so near to giving birth; he was her protector and provider, and he was for the son that was in her womb as well. He could not risk leaving them in Nazareth. He wasn't as comfortable with the neighbor's perceptions of Mary as she seemed to be, and he felt strongly that she should be by his side.

The questions of Mary's heart transitioned into the intercessory petitions of a cherished daughter; *Lord, are You sure that You and the Roman Empire have your timetables coordinated? Nazareth has become comfortable and surely my time is near for the delivery of Your son.* She stopped and pondered and the Lord brought to her memory words that were spoken by the prophet Micah that she had heard spoken in the synagogue and on street corners where rabbis would dialogue with passersby. *"But, as for you, Bethlehem…From you One will go forth for Me to be ruler in Israel. His goings forth are from long ago, from the days of eternity. Therefore He will give them up until the time when she who is in labor has borne a child. Then the remainder of His brethren will return to the sons of Israel. And He will arise and shepherd His flock in the strength of the Lord, in the majesty of the name of the Lord His God. And they will remain, because at that time He will be great to the ends of the earth."*[6]

She humbly bowed her head, remembering that as much as Jehovah loved her, this child and his birth was not just about her, it was about the salvation of many. She pondered these thoughts in her heart for many moments while her tea grew cold and her heart warm. Excitement and faith for the journey began to fill her spirit.

Then, with renewed boldness she added a closing request to the Father above that she loved and trusted, and yet just wanted to be sure He knew her desires. With a smile on her lips she said, *I have just two little requests. Would You please provide a private place for me and Joseph so that we might drink in the wonder of Your gift to us? Also, wherever this child is born, would You please send some minstrels with a song of jubilation? I'd like it very much if the song would match the praise that I have in my heart for You and Your wondrous works.*

Thank You, Father. You're my best friend and closest confidante. I trust You implicitly. As king Solomon wrote so long ago, I know that You have "made everything beautiful in its time."[7] *To walk with You is to be in peace, so off to Bethlehem we go. Truly, "Your word is a lamp to my feet and a light for my path."*[8]

The four-day journey riding on the back of their noble, gentle donkey had been uncomfortable to say the least. However, when she had tried walking part of the journey, her contractions would begin, and she had not wanted to have her baby on a roadside on the way into Bethlehem, especially since there were so many travelers on the same road.

Finally, they made it into Bethlehem only to discover that there were no rooms in any inns available to them. They were exhausted and weary from their long journey. They knew in their hearts, that there must be a place that their heavenly Father had prepared; they just needed to find it. Finally, coming to the last inn at the edge of town, opposite of where they had entered Bethlehem, a generous-hearted inn-keeper and his wife made room for them. They allowed them to stay in a barn just outside the inn where the inn-keeper's cattle and the camels of the guests of the inn normally lodged their animals. Tonight was warm enough for most of the camels to 'lodge' outside in the corral, so *they were welcome to stay*. They were thankful for this humble place, as it provided enough hay for them to rest comfortably.

Joseph had carefully helped her off the donkey and quickly arranged a resting-place for her. He quickly unloaded their few belongings, and then stoked the little fire-pit that the inn-keeper had already started for them just outside the barn. He turned to go outside for one more item and Mary called to him, confessing that she had been having strong, consistent contractions since the moment they entered Bethlehem. Now, they were closer together and very painful. She bid him to go and call for the inn-keeper's wife to come and help her.

It seemed that he was gone forever, as she was alone with two cows, a camel, and three chickens. The pains grew worse and closer together, she had assisted in many neighbor's births growing up and had aided her mother as she helped others to deliver their babies. But she had no idea what the pain of childbirth really felt like until this very moment.

She had turned fifteen before she and Joseph wed, but that was still young. She knew girls who had babies at thirteen, but most were her age or older. All of a sudden, she felt very young and drawn back to her childhood days; they were pain-free. Another pain began; *Joseph, where are you?!*

This pain was more intense than anything she had ever felt; what she really wanted was her mother. *"Oh Lord Jehovah,"* she screamed, *"please help me!"* The chickens startled and ran out of the barn door with feathers flying. The two cows and one camel stood steady.

Instantly, she remembered all the women she had seen give birth that seemed to have an easier time, sat up in a squatting position and breathed short quick breaths in the midst of the contractions. She could hear her mother's voice say, *"Breath over the top of it now...... That's it; that's it..... You can do it.... Good."* She began to say these same words in her mind as the next contraction began, and then she began to "breathe" like the others she had seen in childbirth. She did this over and over again. *What was taking Joseph so long?!*

When Joseph returned with the inn-keepers wife, the pains had intensified to the point that Mary knew it was time for the birth of her son. She called out to Joseph, and the inn-keeper's wife directed him to hold Mary up under her arms as she remained in the sitting position. The inn-keeper's wife, obviously a woman of years and experience, said firmly but calmly, *"Push; my dear sweet girl! ... Push!"* And 'push' she did. Baby Jesus burst upon the scene, into the inn-keeper's wife's waiting arms, with life in his lungs and a cry of victory from his sweet lips.

Mary wept, Joseph wept, the inn-keepers wife wept—all with tears of joy. The cows mooed and the camel snorted in seeming delight. The inn-keeper's wife held baby Jesus up for Mary and Joseph to see. Joseph then laid Mary down carefully and went to her side and embraced her with joy. The inn-keeper's wife quickly attended to the umbilical cord, and then told Mary to give her one more big push. All was well. She then quickly washed him in water and rubbed him in salt, and wrapped him in fresh swaddling cloths and handed him to his mother.[9] While Joseph and Mary looked adoringly at their firstborn son, she finished cleaning the birthing area, and then graciously left the young family to enjoy their time together. It was a beautiful private place, hidden away from the hustle and bustle of the world outside.

He did not open his eyes until Mary gently stroked his perfect little hand, saying, *"Welcome, baby Jesus. Welcome to this world and to our family. You are so amazing; so perfect!"* He looked up at her and almost smiled as she said, *"I love you little boy, and I dedicate myself completely to you."* He then nestled into her closely and Mary opened her tunic and nursed him by her side. She and Joseph looked at each other in wonder and awe at the miracle she held in her arms.

The mooing of the cows was the lullaby that wooed baby Jesus to sleep that night. Somewhere in the echo of the heavens they could almost hear angels singing praises to God in the highest for the birth of His Son. Indeed, angels were singing praises to God, proclaiming His goodness to the shepherds on a nearby hillside.

Have you ever been confused about the events in your life and then suddenly realized the hand of God was at work? Have you ever been so amazed at your thoughts concerning your child that you dare not do anything more than ponder them in your heart? Have you ever thought that if people really knew what you could see in your child, they would dismiss you as a foolish, nearsighted woman? Have you ever marveled so at the goodness of God that you were left speechless and contemplative?

That is what it must have been like for Mary. God was so ordering her steps that every detail was seemingly outlined to the minutest detail.

At census time, all male adults were required to return to the headquarters of their ancestral tribe and register. Joseph, being of the house of David, would have had his familial headquarters in Bethlehem. Although ancient census records show that people had to return to their hometowns for a tax census, the city to which they returned was also where they owned property, not simply where they were born. Not only had Joseph likely been born and raised in Bethlehem, but he also possibly owned property there. This would have been considered his legal residence, even though he lived in Nazareth. One copy of an actual government edict from Egypt reads:

> Gaius Vibius Maximus, Prefect of Egypt, orders: "Seeing that the time has come for the house-to-house census, it is necessary to compel all those who for any cause whatsoever are residing

outside their districts to return to their own homes, that they may both carry out the regular order of the census, and may also diligently attend to the cultivation of their allotments." [10]

Although the tax laws in most of the Roman Empire required only the head of a household to appear, women over the age of 12 were also taxed. Mary would not have been required to appear to register, but Joseph must not have wanted to leave her behind with the time of birth so near.

When you consider the increased traffic a census would have brought into little Bethlehem, it would be easy to imagine that people were murmuring about Rome's oppression, as well as the burden of taxation and inconvenience of travel. All of this murmuring and complaining would have been going on while a Savior was being born in their midst. Often while we're complaining, God is at work.

Often while we're complaining, God is at work.

Inns with no vacancy would be prophetically symbolic of what was to happen to Jesus. One day in the future, the only place for Him would be on a cross. How often do we, as mothers, get so consumed and overcrowded in our schedules that we miss the birth of Christ in our daily lives? How often do we relegate Him to a lonely cross?

Hundreds of years prior to this time, Micah proclaimed, *"But, you Bethlehem…out of you will come for me one who will be ruler over Israel, whose origins are from of old, from ancient times"* (Mic. 5:2). For Jesus to be born in busy little Bethlehem would fulfill this prophecy and establish His covenant connection with David.

So the steps of Joseph and Mary were ordered to bring about this fulfillment. Why Mary? Why Bethlehem? Why now? Because God had so ordered it; her steps were on His timetable.

How many mothers do you know whose children came at the "wrong" time? According to your plans, were you one of those mothers or one of those children? That would have been the testimony of a friend of mine a few years ago. She is a single mother of two beautiful children. One of her children seemed to have arrived at the perfect time; the other arrived at a time that would have baffled most.

My friend was married to a wonderful, sensitive, talented man who was full of life and had a gift to teach. Their marriage had some of the typical problems that most young marriages have, but they were happy. The main point of frustration for her was her inability to conceive. She desperately wanted to experience the joy of motherhood.

After making the decision to place herself under medical supervision, she began to take fertility drugs. Much to her delight one day the news came that they were to have a child. Her husband came home with two dozen roses in hand. Several months later they were blessed with the life of their first child. God had indeed worked a miracle.

Although their first child was a constant joy to them, this young mother began to earnestly desire to have another child. Much to her dismay, the months and years continued to turn over as easily as the pages on a calendar.

Unknown to her, her husband had begun to struggle in other areas in his life. It seemed that an encompassing fog of despair overcame the sunshine of their home. She tried to hold fast to the dreams within their grasp, but her husband's hand began to slip from hers. Sadness entered where there had once been joy; frustration replaced love; confusion conquered the peace that was once theirs.

It was the fall season when he left. How appropriate it seemed. Leaves were falling and so was their hope. The sparkle of love and dreams that once filled their hearts seemed illusive and unreachable. They tried to reach each other, but the love that once burned brightly was obscured by many hurtful choices.

Unending questions plagued her days and nights. *Were there no more miracles to be discovered? Were there no more hidden riches yet to be revealed? Was there a miracle to be found in the approaching Christmas season?*

Her monthly cycle had been so irregular with all of the recent stress that she hadn't given its absence much thought. But then there was this feeling inside of her. *Could it be? Surely not.* She decided to restore her peace of mind by purchasing a pregnancy test.

Much to her surprise and delight, new life was once again within her womb. Initially, she was thrilled with the miracle inside of her. But to her great sorrow, her now ex-husband's response was *Why now?* He was gone emotionally and now physically from their once beautiful marriage.

After the birth of her child, as she realized how complicated her life had become, she too wondered about the Lord's timing. *What was this miracle that lay resting in her arms? Why now, in the midst of a broken marriage covenant?*

The answer to her ponderings would be the same as Mary's: because God so ordered it; her steps were on His timetable. She, like Mary, would see that "No eye has seen, no ear has heard, no mind has conceived what God has prepared for those who love Him" (1 Cor. 2:9; Isa. 64:4).

She would find this great Shepherd to be faithful where there had been unfaithfulness, understanding where there had been misunderstanding, and caring where there had been neglect. She would not be removed from her reality, but she would be swept into His all-encompassing grace, time and time again.

Did she wonder about the timing and possible destiny of this child? Yes, she did. Were her meditations many? Yes, they were. But along with Mary, it was in this specific truth—that God had so ordered it and she was on His timetable—that her hope found a place to abide. The birth of this child was in God's perfect timing.

Do you ever wonder about the timing and possible destiny of your child? Are your meditations many? Listen closely and see if you can hear the meditations of your child's heart. Does your child sing to the Lord with David of old?

Oh yes, you shaped me first inside, then out; you formed me in my mother's womb. I thank you, High God—you're breathtaking! Body and soul, I am marvelously made! I worship in adoration— what a creation! You know me inside and out, you know every bone in my body; You know exactly how I was made, bit by bit, how I was sculpted from nothing into something. Like an open book, you watched me grow from conception to birth; all the stages of my life were spread out before you, the days of my life all prepared before I'd even lived one day. Your thoughts—how rare, how beautiful! God, I'll never comprehend them! I couldn't even begin to count them—any more than I could count the sand of the sea. Oh, let me rise in the morning and live always with you! (Ps. 139:13-18, *The Message Bible*)

What a song, what a proclamation! Why me, you ask? Why this child, and why now? Because God has so ordered it, and you are on His timetable. You are His "highly favored one" for this specific child at this specific time. His promise to you is, as it was to Mary so many years ago, "No eye has seen, no ear has heard, no mind has conceived what God has prepared for those who love him" (1 Cor.2:9). It is in this truth that your hope can find a place to abide.

You are His "highly favored one" for this specific child at this specific time.

Shepherding was not considered an honorable trade in the Jewish culture in Mary's day. It was a very demanding trade. Because of this the shepherds were unable to keep the details of the Jewish ceremonial laws. All of the meticulous hand-washing rules and regulations were beyond the demands of their daily lifestyle. Even participation in the normal religious activities of their communities was uncommon for them.

Because they were nomadic, they were also assumed to be the thieves when local sheep were missing. They were commonly categorized as "sinners" among their own people. I wonder if God sent the angels to the shepherds first as an indication of the sinners to whom He was sending His Son.

It is possible that the shepherds the angels visited were the shepherds who watched over the flocks destined for Temple sacrifices at Passover. Just think! Those tending the Passover lambs would be among the first to see the Lamb of God, who would be the sacrificial lamb for the sins of the world. It was to these humble sinners that the song of jubilation and revelation would come and to whom the Lamb of God would be revealed.

If Mary had been disappointed that there were no earthly minstrels to sing with jubilation when her son was born, she would be blessed to hear the reports that angels had sung the song that no earthly singer could. This song of praise was beyond anything she could have imagined.

The Archoko Volume chronicles a written interview of the shepherds by a young man named Jonathan who was a servant to a Jewish priest in Bethlehem at the time. Here is a portion of his report to the Sanhedrin:

When they were aroused, it was light as day but they knew it was not daylight, for it was only the third watch. All at once the air seemed to be filled with human voices, saying, "Glory! Glory! Glory to the most high God!" and "Happy art thou, Bethlehem, for God hath fulfilled His promise to the fathers; for in thy chambers is born the King that shall rule in righteousness." Their shoutings would rise up in the heavens and then would sink down in mellow strains and roll along at the foot of the mountains, and die away in the most soft and musical manner they had ever heard; then it would begin again high up in the heavens, in the very vaults of the sky, and descend in sweet and melodious strains, so that they could not refrain from shouting and weeping at the same time. The light would seem to burst forth high up in the heavens, and then descend in softer rays, and light up the hills and valleys, making everything more visible than the light of the sun, though it was not so brilliant, but clearer, like the brightest moon......I asked them how they felt—if they were not afraid; they said at first they were, but after a while it seemed to calm their spirits, and so fill their hearts with love and tranquility that they felt more like giving thanks than anything else.[11]

This specific account is a historical record, not a Biblical one. So whether the details are accurate or not, we do not know. However, from the biblical account in Luke, we do know that what the shepherds reported to Mary (and Joseph) caused her to quietly ponder their words in her heart. We also know the shepherds spread the word throughout Bethlehem and "all who heard it were amazed at what the shepherds said to them" (Luke 2:18). We also know they "returned, glorifying and praising God for all the things they had heard and seen, which were just as they had been told" (Luke 2:20).

There was another mother in contemporary Church history who had things to ponder about one of her children. Her name was Sarah Mumford. Having lost three infant sons to death by the time her only daughter, Catherine, was born, she considered her to be a very special gift.

Catherine was a very active and observant child who had a keen imagination. Without being formally taught, she quickly learned her letters and could read by the age of three. She so loved the exciting stories of the Bible that by the time she was twelve years old she had read it through eight times.

One day Catherine was so intrigued by the story of young Samuel hearing God's call that she asked her mother, "Did the Lord ever speak in such a way to a little girl like me?" Her mother smiled and began to tell her the story in 2 Kings 5:1-14. She said, "That part of history tells us that Naaman, the head of the Syrian army, suffered from the dreadful disease of leprosy. Naaman's wife had a Jewish slave girl. This little maid was impressed by the Lord to tell her mistress that her husband could be healed if he would go to the prophet Elisha and follow his instructions."

She continued the story of how Naaman obeyed the prophet and washed seven times in the Jordan River. She said, "When he came out of the water, the Bible says that his 'flesh came again like the flesh of a little child, and he was clean.'"

At this point young Catherine looked at her own clear skin and asked, "Could God work through another little girl in our time?"

"Of course," replied her mother.

"Even a little girl like me?"

"Yes, even a little girl like you."

Another time, while doing one of her daily chores of carrying in a fresh supply of wood for the household fire, Catherine asked, "Mama, will the Lord answer my prayers?"

"Of course. Why do you ask?" her mother responded.

"Because there are so many things in this world that are wrong. There are children who have to go to bed without having anything to eat all day. Think, Mama, how simply dreadful it must be to go to bed hungry!" Wiping away tears, she continued, "I almost wish I could give my portion of the cake to a poor family I know."

Today we know that this young, tenderhearted girl went on to become the cofounder of the Salvation Army, alongside her husband William Booth. Her husband often asked her to help him with his sermons, as he was known to say, "You know the Bible better than I do." As a speaker, she filled some of the largest auditoriums in England. She wrote books and became the "mother" of this "army" that still feeds and clothes the poor today. [12]

I wonder if her mother pondered Catherine's thought-provoking questions long after their discussions ended. I wonder if she ever dreamed that her daughter would write, speak to thousands and be responsible for sharing the love of Christ with so many poor in such practical ways. I wonder if she ever imagined that the influence of her daughter's life would cross the ocean to another continent. I wonder if she wondered. Do you wonder about your children?

I have a friend named Randi who became a grandmother for the first time a few years ago. Interestingly enough, she is one of the great-grand-daughters of William and Catherine Booth, by an extended-family relationship. She, like Catherine's mother, Sarah Mumford, has much to ponder about her children.

One evening around the dinner table at a pastors gathering, she shared recent photos and the delights of her new role as a grandmother. She concluded our conversation by saying, "My cup of blessing is full." With a look of wonder and a tear in her eye she repeated, "My cup of blessing is full." Not only had she meditated on the wonder of God in the lives of her children when they were young, but now she was also pondering the goodness of God in their adult years.

She has three young adult children. They're all married now, but it is the oldest one who presented her with the title of grandmother first. All of her children are actively serving the Lord; indeed, her "cup of blessing is full."

When she made this statement, I was reminded of a story I heard her second son, Jason, tell in a college chapel service. He said that when he was just a little guy he loved to walk to the store with his mother and hold her hand.

As they walked along, Jason would slip his hand out of his mother's and say, "You're not holding on tight enough, Mommy." She would smile and once again take hold of his hand. He would wait awhile and then slip his hand out of her trusting grasp and scold, "You're not holding on tight enough." She would chuckle and say, "Okay," and take his hand once again. When his hand was unable to find its momentary release, he would adoringly commend her, "That's good, Mommy."

This was part of their familiar journey to the store and back. It was a playful ritual of enduring trust and loving assurance of a mother's care for her son. Through the years she held tightly to her God and taught her children how to do so as well.

While in college, Jason became a mentor to other children, teaching them how to hold tightly to the hand of God. Like Catherine Booth, he too had a desire to reach out to those in need. He held the hands of those in need by reaching out to children raised in inner-city neighborhoods. I wonder what he pondered as he took hold of their trusting hands. I wonder if they too slipped their hands away as an inquisitive test. The lesson of trust engraved on his own heart is one he then etched onto the hearts of others.

Jason's mother, Randi, had simple, yet profound, thoughts concerning all of her children. She faithfully brought those ponderings before the Lord in prayer many times over the years. In doing so, she transformed her meditations into fruitfulness through the lives of her children and grandchildren.

How precious, how sweet are the ponderings of mothers, both young and old. How faithful and how prolific, as a mother's meditations become intercessions, and intercessions become fruit that feeds a generation—all for the Master's use.

How faithful and how prolific, as a mother's meditations become intercessions, and intercessions become fruit that feeds a generation—all for the Master's use.

You may not have shepherds coming to tell you of angelic proclamations concerning your children, but join in the chorus and herald the good news: "Glory to God in the highest, and on earth peace to men [and women] on whom His favor rests" (Luke 2:14).

His favor rests with you. Treasure up all these things and ponder them in your heart, for these unspoken treasures are your hidden riches both now and in the years to come. Cherish them as you would a family heirloom. If you do, you may find that your spirit will sing in chorus with Randi's, "My cup of blessing is full."

The Timetable of the Lord

PSALM 31:15: *"My times are in Your hand; deliver me from the hand of my enemies and from those who persecute me." (NASB)*

PSALM 27:5: *"For in the time of trouble He shall hide me in His pavilion: In the secret place of His tabernacle He shall hide me; He shall set me high upon a rock." (NKJV)*

PSALM 37:39: *"But the salvation of the righteous is from the Lord; He is their strength in the time of trouble." (NKJV)*

PSALM 113:2: *"Blessed be the name of the Lord from this time forth and forevermore!" (NKJV)*

PSALM 121:8: *"The Lord shall preserve your going out and your coming in from this time forth, and even forevermore." (NKJV)*

ECCLESIASTES 3:1-8: *"There is an appointed time for everything, and there is a time for every event under heaven—a time to give birth and a time to die; a time to plant and a time to uproot what is planted. A time to kill and a time to heal; a time to tear down and a time to build up. A time to weep and a time to laugh; a time to mourn and a time to dance. A time to throw stones and a time to gather stones; a time to embrace and a time to shun embracing. A time to search and a time to give up as lost; a time to keep and time to throw away. A time to tear apart and a time to sew together; a time to be silent and a time to speak. A time to love and a time to hate; a time for war and a time for peace." (NASB)*

NOTES

1   *"Virginity is a virtue in the creation-law order for three reasons at least: (1) It was commanded to keep the monogamous relationship of marriage undefiled (Exod 22); (2) Marriage of a man with a virgin insured the purity of the inheritance which was fundamentally important to the sacerdotal offices of specific groups within Israel (Lev 21:14); (3) Virginity was considered in and of itself to be a desirable state (Esth 2:2, et al.). Accordingly, loss of virginity was to be within the bounds of marriage and loss through force a severe misfortune (2 Sam 13:13,14).* General Editor Merrill C. Tenney, Associate Editor Steven Barabas, *The Zondervan Pictorial Encyclopedia of the Bible, Volume Five Q-Z,* (Zondervan Publishing House, A Division of Harper Collins Publishers, Grand Rapids, Michigan, 1975, 1976 by The Zondervan Corporation), p. 885.

2   *"The bride's parents had the responsibility to preserve the 'tokens of virginity' of their daughter, the blood-stained garment or sheet from the nuptial bed. Such proofs were preserved as proper evidence in case the husband accused his wife of unchastity. In the case that he was found to be a liar he was first whipped, then fined twice the amount of a normal dowry (Deut 22:13-19). However, if the accusations were true the wife was stoned (22:20,21).* General Editor Merrill C. Tenney, Associate Editor Steven Barabas, *The Zondervan Pictorial Encyclopedia of the Bible, Volume Four M-P,* (Zondervan Publishing House, A Division of Harper Collins Publishers, Grand Rapids, Michigan, 1975, 1976 by The Zondervan Corporation), p. 100.

3   *"I adorned you with ornaments, put bracelets on your wrists, and a chain on your neck. And I put a jewel in your nose, earrings in your ears, and a beautiful crown on your head. Thus you were adorned with gold and silver, and your clothing was of fine linen, silk, and embroidered cloth..."* Ezekiel 16:11-13 NKJV

4   *"The headwear consists of a tall pear-embroidered triangle, framed by a garland of fresh flowers and branches of rue, believed to ward off the evil eye." Women in Judaism, Class 9 – The Eternal Jewish Bride: A Survey of Jewish Marriage Customs, Women in Judaism – Torah.org,* http://www.torah.org/learning/women/class9.html (May 28, 2004,).
"Rue is...known as the Herb of Repentance. It has also been referred to as the plant of patience and endurance as one rue plant could live for hundreds of years. It symbolizes virginity and plays an important role in wedding ceremonies. The bride usually wears a wreath of rue." Meanings & Legends of Flowers ®, copyright@ Pinkie D'Cruz 1998, Meaning & Legends of Flowers – R, http://www.angelfire.com/journal2/flowers/r.html (May 28,2004).
"Rue is a plant or shrub, which in Mediterranean countries grows from 90cm to 1.5m tall and has yellowish flowers and strong-smelling leaves. Both species grow wild in Palestine and Syria and were probably also cultivated there in N.T. times. Rue was used as a condiment, and its fresh leaves were used to heal certain diseases, insect stings and snake bites." Fauna and Flora of the Bible, Helps for Translators, Volume XI, (United Bible Societies, U.S.A., 1972), p.174.

5   *"On the eve of the wedding the bride was led from her family home to that of her husband. First there was music, then a distribution of wine and oil among the people and nuts among the children. Next came the bride covered by the bridal veil and surrounded by her companions. Some carried torches or lamps or flowers. Everyone along the way applauded the procession or joined it. When the bride arrived at the home of the bridegroom, she was led to her husband, and the bride and groom were crowned with garlands. A formal legal instrument was signed, in which the groom promised to care for and keep his wife in the manner of the men of Israel. There were benedictions and the prescribed washing of hands, followed by the marriage feast, at which the guests contributed to the general enjoyment."* Howard F. Vos, *Nelson's New Illustrated Bible Manners & Customs,* (Thomas Nelson Publishers, Nashville, Tennessee, 1999), p, 449.

6   Micah 5:2-4 NASB

7   Eccl. 3:11 NKJV

8   Ps. 119:105 NKJV

9   Albert Barnes, *Barnes' Notes on the New Testament,* (Grand Rapids, Michigan 49503, Kregel Publications, 1962, 1963, 1966), p. 189.

10 William Barclay, *The Daily Study Bible, The Gospel of Luke* (Edinburgh: The Saint Andrew Press, 1975), p. 21.

11 Drs. McIntosh and Twyman, *The Archko Volume or the Archeological Writings of the Sanhedrin and Talmuds of the Jews* (New Canaan, Conn.: Keats Publishing, 1975), p. 65.

12 Charles Ludwig, *Mother of an Army,* (Minneapolis: Bethany House Publishers, 1987), p. 15.

The Early Year of Preparation

A Mother's First Release

When the time of their purification according to the Law of Moses had been completed, Joseph and Mary took him to Jerusalem to present him to the Lord (as it is written in the Law of the Lord, "Every firstborn male is to be consecrated to the Lord"), and to offer a sacrifice in keeping with what is said in the Law of the Lord: "a pair of doves or two young pigeons." Now there was a man in Jerusalem called Simeon, who was righteous and devout. He was waiting for the consolation of Israel, and the Holy Spirit was upon him. It had been revealed to him by the Holy Spirit that he would not die before he had seen the Lord's Christ. Moved by the Spirit, he went into the temple courts. When the parents brought in the child Jesus to do for him what the custom of the Law required, Simeon took him in his arms and praised God, saying: "Sovereign Lord, as you have promised, you now dismiss your servant in peace. For my eyes have seen your salvation, which you have prepared in the sight of all people, a light for revelation to the Gentiles and for glory to your people Israel." The child's father and mother marveled at what was said about him. Then Simeon blessed them and said to Mary, his mother: "This child is destined to cause the falling and rising of many in Israel, and to be a sign that will be spoken against, so that the thoughts of many hearts will be revealed. And a sword will pierce your own soul too." — Luke 2:22-35

Thirty-two days had passed since Mary and Joseph had taken the baby to the local synagogue where he was circumcised and then officially received his name. They did this in obedience to what God had told Abram long ago, "For the generations to come every male among you who is eight days old must be circumcised." [1] This message had been engraved in their hearts since childhood, and they responded appropriately on this important day of their son's life.

Although, according to their custom, because Mary was still considered ceremonially impure at the time of this important event, she rejoiced from a distance during the sacred ceremony. This was the day that signified her son's covenant with God as an individual on His own. He had been in her arms a mere eight days and now she had released Him back to Jehovah to begin His new cycle of life, not from within her, but from without.

Now, her day of ceremonial purification had finally arrived. [2] The past 40 days had been days of quiet awe and special bonding with her newborn son, and yet it was amazing how long 40 days could seem when you were inside virtually every hour of the day. She actually was enjoying being out in the fresh air again. Jerusalem was only six miles from Bethlehem, a pleasant two-hour journey. The sun was shining and felt good on her face, while the clop of the donkey's hooves was like a soothing melody to her ears. He was moving gently along as Joseph walked and led him by the twined harness, and baby Jesus rested in her arms swaddled in his ecru cloth and purple blanket.

She and Joseph had carefully selected and purchased the two pigeons that they would offer the priest as a burnt offering and sin offering. They were in a cage attached to a two-wheeled pull-cart that Joseph built, which was attached and pulled behind the back of the donkey. It was important for the pigeons to be perfect, without any blemish or they would be found to be unworthy sacrifices, so Mary and Joseph had been especially careful in their selection. She knew that Jehovah would accept her offering, but she prayed that the priest would as well.

Not only was this her day of purification, but it was a special day for baby Jesus as well. Today he would experience the ceremony of The Redemption of the Firstborn. How exciting it was to fulfill the word the Lord had spoken to Moses so long ago: "Consecrate to me every firstborn male. The first offspring of every womb among the Israelites belongs to me..." [3]

The wonder of the ensuing ceremony filled her mind. As the baby slept quietly in her arms, her thoughts quickly turned into mindful intercessions. *Oh Lord Jehovah, my heart is so full on this day. What wonders You have performed! Thank You that I can publicly present my child to You in your Holy Temple today. Everyday I offer him to You, but this day is special, Lord. It's Your day; it's my day, it's his day – it's ours. Thank You Father, for Your redemption!*

Joseph looked back as he tuned into the sound of her voice and gave her a knowing smile. He too was offering prayers up to the Lord as he walked, guiding the donkey so carefully. Assured that she and the baby were okay, he turned back to focus on the road ahead. Oh, how she loved him. *What a kind and gentle husband You have given me, Lord. Though we are not rich in worldly goods, we are rich in love and in Your goodness. Thank you for Joseph, this wonderful man who not only hears Your voice, but obeys it as well. Help me to be a good wife to him all of his days.*

Prepare my heart, Lord, to hear Your voice today. Tell me more, Father, about this child. Baby Jesus wiggled in her arms, opening his eyes in response to the sound of her voice. With his brown curly hair edging it's way out of his swaddling cloth and his beautiful brown eyes looking into hers, she cooed at him adoringly, and then nestled him close while rocking him in her arms until his eyes closed once again. As his eyes closed, she continued, *yes oh Lord, tell me more about this precious son. Guide me in the way I should go. Grant unto me insight and wisdom upon this day of complete surrender and dedication to You.*

A whispered psalm from heaven above dropped into her heart, *"I will also appoint him my firstborn, the most exalted of the kings of the earth. I will maintain my love to him forever, and my covenant with him will never fail. I will establish his line forever, his throne as long as the heavens endure."*[4] With deep gratitude, she began to weep and offer praises to the Lord. Once again, Joseph looked back to attend to any needs that she may have, but realizing that she was wholly in the presence of Jehovah, he returned his eyes to the road ahead and began to praise the God of heaven with an undivided heart.

The presence of God ministered to Mary's heart on the road that day. Even before they got to the Temple, He prepared her for the next step in her journey.

Can you identify with Mary? Have you ever looked at your child and wondered what the Lord had in mind when He created this little one and placed him or her in your arms? Have you ever wondered what really took place from God's perspective when you offered your child back in dedication to Him? Have you ever wondered what you and the Lord would do together with that offering?

In Mary's day it was the Jewish custom for a woman who had given birth to be considered ceremonially impure for a season of time. She could go about her household chores and daily business, but she could not participate in any religious ceremonies nor could she enter the Temple. If she had given birth to a baby boy, this period was for 40 days. If it was a girl, it was for 80 days.

At the end of this time she had to bring to the Temple a lamb, or two doves or pigeons if she was poor. This was offered up as a sin offering unto the Lord. At this same time she was allowed to present the child to the priest to be publicly presented to the Lord.

This presentation was not a redemptive act that cleansed the child from sin; rather it was a consecration of the child to the Lord. It was an act of setting the child aside for a special purpose, deeming the child as holy to the Lord.

In Protestant religions today, new mothers are not considered to be impure after the birth of a child. However, they usually bring their new little one to the house of the Lord to present the baby, not only to their friends but also to the Lord. Many churches have a ceremony in which they dedicate the child to the Lord, symbolic of consecrating the child to the Lord's purposes.

A baby's ceremonial dedication is not considered as a sacrament of the Church. However, it is more than a mere extension of Judaism; it is also evidenced in Scripture throughout the ministry of Jesus. Mothers often brought their children to Him to receive His rabbinical blessing as He traveled from place to place, preaching the good news of the kingdom of God. Surely this is a pattern for us today, just as the rest of His earthly walk was.

After observing baby dedication ceremonies many times through the years, I have made a few observations. Babies who are placed into a pastor's unfamiliar arms and positioned closely to his booming voice are often startled by the adult world around them. They may look like they're lifting their arms to praise the Lord, but they're really not.

Actually, this whole process, though sacred is risky for all involved. If the baby is handed over to the minister in a familiar feeding position and this person is ill equipped to meet that need, you're bound to have a screaming baby for the duration of the dedicatory prayer. When a mother hands her baby to the minister, it's also best not to hand him or her over when they are wet or hungry. For that matter, if the baby has recently been fed and not burped, the minister and the baby could be on the brink of momentary disaster rather than holy bonding!

When Mary, Joseph and baby Jesus arrived in Jerusalem, they met a man named Simeon, even before they got inside the Temple doors. The Lord had promised Simeon that he would not die until he had seen the Lord's Christ. This day, Simeon had been led by the Holy Spirit to go to the Temple.

Simeon was known as one of "the quiet of the land." These were people who were known for waiting quietly and patiently on God for the revelation of the Messiah. They believed in a life of constant prayer and quiet watchfulness until He would come. Simeon was in tune with the prophetic revelation of the coming of the Messiah as outlined in the last four verses of Daniel 9. [5]

Seventy "sevens" are decreed for your people and your holy city to finish transgression, to put an end to sin, to atone for wickedness, to bring in everlasting righteousness, to seal up vision and prophecy and to anoint the most holy. Know and understand this: From the issuing of the decree to restore and rebuild Jerusalem until the Anointed One, the ruler, comes, there will be seven "sevens," and sixty-two "sevens." It will be rebuilt with streets and a trench, but in times of trouble. After the sixty-two "sevens." The Anointed One will be cut off and will have nothing. The people of the ruler who will come will destroy the city and the sanctuary. The end will come like a flood: War will continue until the end, and desolations have been decreed. He will confirm a covenant with many for one "seven." In the middle of the "seven" he will put an end to sacrifice and offering. And on a wing of the temple he will set up an abomination that causes desolation, until the end that is decreed is poured out on him.

Simeon's spirit must have been filled with this passage of Scripture as he prophesied, "Sovereign Lord as you have promised, you now dismiss your servant in peace. For my eyes have seen your salvation, which you have prepared in the sight of all people, a light for revelation to the Gentiles and for glory to your people Israel." [6] Little did he know that the first sermon Jesus would preach some 30 years later would be, "The time has come...," [7] as a fulfillment of Daniel 9:24-27.

Simeon blessed Mary and Joseph and the babe, and then spoke directly to Mary: "This child is destined to cause the falling and rising of many in Israel, and to be a sign that will be spoken against, so that the thoughts of many hearts will be revealed. And a sword will pierce your own soul too." [8]

Just as Simeon finished speaking, an aged woman, who was a prophetess named Anna, came up to them. When she saw the babe, she began to praise God and preach about the child to all those around who also had been watching and waiting.

What mind-numbing, spirit-invigorating moments those must have been. Can you imagine? While prophetess Anna was starting praise parties all around and Simeon was departing to go to his final resting place in peace, I can only imagine that Mary was contemplating Simeon's closing words to her as well as the statements about her Savior and son. *A sword will pierce your own soul too, Mary.* I wonder if she was still pondering those words as she and Joseph entered the Temple to make their offerings and consecrate Jesus to the Lord. I doubt that she dismissed them carelessly; I imagine that they remained pocketed in her heart for the next three decades and more.

There will be many blessings spoken to you throughout your motherhood journey; there may also be words that will pierce your own soul too. There will be Simeons to whom you will look for encouragement and enlightenment. They will faithfully offer you both, even though sometimes their words will unsettle your soul.

There will be many blessings spoken to you throughout your motherhood journey; there may also be words that will pierce your own soul too.

Julia, a friend of mine, has heard the message of the ancient Simeon right through her own soul numerous times in recent years. She and her husband, Steve, are the parents of two beautiful healthy children, Michael and Rebekah. The angels didn't sing, and the magi didn't visit at their births; but their parent-hearts rejoiced, and God did indeed provide all their needs.

As the years passed after the birth of their second child, Julia longed to have more children. Finally, when Michael and Rebekah were 12 and 10, she received the good news that she was expecting again.

However, their joy ended in an unexpected miscarriage. The loss of this new life was overwhelming, especially when it was learned that the child in the womb was not one, but three—a set of triplets. Truly, a sword had pierced Julia's soul at the loss of this triple blessing. Within the next year, healing came and with it the news that she was expecting again.

Prior to the birth of this child, a question had come to Julia's mind several times over a three-year period: "Would you still be willing to have another baby if you knew something would be wrong with it?" Believing this to be from the Lord because it produced no fear in her she would conversationally respond, "Okay. But if You ask me to do this, I'm going to ask You for grace. I'll say 'yes' because I believe that You only give good gifts."

Although this conversation went on in Julia's heart a number of times, she felt no fear throughout this pregnancy. Each time she prayed, the reassuring thought came to her, *"I'm going to be with you."*

There were no reasons for the doctors to be concerned about Julia or her baby, as everything appeared to be developing along completely normally, so no ultrasounds or other extra tests were requested. However, due to an alarming dream prior to the birth of her new child, Julia and her husband made the decision to prepare Michael and Rebekah, now 14 and 12, for the possibility of the birth of a handicapped child. Both children wholeheartedly responded, "Mom, it doesn't matter. We will love the baby no matter what."

When Julia's labor began, everyone was excited. However, during the time of labor and delivery, both Julia and her new baby girl almost died in the delivery process. Immediately after the birth of baby Elizabeth, the doctors and nurses quickly moved her to another room. Although Steve wanted to stay by Julia's side to watch over her, Julia sensed that her baby's life was in danger and insisted that he follow the doctors.

Tiny Elizabeth was simply not responding to life. Doctors and nurses filled the room in a panic of activity. When Steve asked if he could pray for his baby, the doctors stepped back, and within 30 seconds Elizabeth was breathing normally again. Stunned, the doctors and nurses stood with tear-filled eyes and wonder in their hearts for what seemed an eternal moment. This would be the first of many miracles in Elizabeth's life.

All babies have eight separate pieces of skull bone in their heads at the time of birth. The bones are separated to enable the baby's skull to overlap so that they can come through the birth canal successfully. One in 180,000 babies is born with one of these skull pieces fused together. Baby Elizabeth had all eight bones fused together at the time of her birth.

The doctor had broken little Elizabeth's skull during the birth process. Although this injury, plus the trauma of birth, put her life in immediate danger, it was the breaking of her skull that actually saved her life in the next few weeks. It also prevented her from being blind and mentally retarded, as the unyielding skull would have damaged the optic nerve and hindered the brain from developing normally. It's amazing how God uses every "breaking" in our lives to release a miracle, both spiritually and naturally.

It's amazing how God uses every "breaking" in our lives to release a miracle, both spiritually and naturally.

Although Julia was thankful for the new life God had placed into her hands, she was in shock in the hours following Elizabeth's birth. She recalls the feeling that even with the preparation God had given her, a person is never prepared for a severely deformed child.

The doctors were her Simeons. They began to tell her of their wonder at the miracle of Elizabeth's birth, yet they predicted the numerous painful challenges that lay ahead for her. Julia went to sleep that first night thinking of the many surgeries her little girl would have to face. In that moment, her heart was woven with Mary's when Mary had stood at the steps of the Temple and Simeon said, "A sword will pierce your own soul, too."

When Elizabeth was four days old, the doctor spoke to Steve and Julia about the first surgery she would need in just a few weeks. He had performed the surgery only once and knew of no other doctors in the nation who had ever done this kind of surgery. This was another sword in Julia's soul—a special child in her arms that no one really knew how to care for.

When Elizabeth was two weeks old, they took her to another specialist in another city to acquire a second opinion on the timing of the upcoming surgery. He agreed with the first doctor and coldly said, "I'd just take that skull off, throw it in the garbage and let her grow a new one." Julia was stunned at his seeming lack of care for the value of Elizabeth's life.

At 2:00 A.M. that morning, Julia picked up the *Gideon Bible* in the motel room and read, "As thou knowest not what is the way of the spirit, *nor how the bones do grow in the womb of her that is with child:* even so thou knowest not the works of God who maketh all." [9] Once again the gentle whispers of the Lord were engraved on her heart. Once again her faith was renewed. Just to be reminded that the Lord was Elizabeth's creator and He was watching over them restored her courage.

When Elizabeth was five weeks old, it was time for her first surgery. The night before the surgery, Julia cherished every moment with her baby, not knowing if Elizabeth would live or die. She recalls the hardest thing was when she handed the baby over to the doctors. Her only consolation was that in doing so, she was not merely handing Elizabeth over to a human doctor, but she was giving her into the hands of the Lord.

The doctors removed little Elizabeth's skull from her eyebrows to the back of her neck. It was a long nine-hour surgery. Although it was successful, she had another minor surgery only one week later. Elizabeth needed 24 hour monitoring. It was truly intensive care on the home front. Her life would be a constant blessing and challenge, not only to her mother but also to her entire family as they each participated in watching over her.

When it came time to officially present her to the Lord at a ceremony of dedication at church, Julia and Steve were well practiced in handing their daughter over to the Lord and into the hands of others. They did so with joy and anticipation of future miracles for this very special daughter.

When Elizabeth was 15 months old, the doctors needed to remove her complete skull so that the developing brain would have room to grow. This surgery was six months earlier than previously planned. Once again this precious mother found her emotions struggling with the piercing sword. "Oh, God, not more pain for Elizabeth. So soon? Why now?" This time Philippians 1:6 rang within her soul: "He who began a good work in you will carry it on to completion."

By now Elizabeth was walking. She would need to wear a helmet, following the surgery, to protect her head. Although her head was physically deformed, her intelligence was not; and she would not like the confinement of the helmet—another challenge for all involved. At a time of further extensive hospital testing and a minor surgery when Elizabeth was two and a half years old, the Lord graciously reassured Julia of His care. He then led her to the verse, "He that goeth forth and weepeth, bearing precious seed, shall doubtless come again with rejoicing, bringing his sheaves with him." [10]

Elizabeth will face another surgery when she is five and again when she is six. She is a bright and intelligent child and is a delight to everyone who comes in contact with her. Oh yes, there are those who are initially shocked by her physical appearance, but then they meet with her winsome smile and can hardly resist giving a smile in return.

There were those who would also look upon Mary's child one day and proclaim, "He grew up before him like a tender shoot, and like a root out of dry ground. He had no beauty or majesty to attract us to him, nothing in his appearance that we should desire him." [11] Yes, these two mothers, Mary and Julia, have been woven together in a great tapestry that reaches across the generations.

American poet Carl Sandburg once said, "A baby is God's opinion that the world should go on." [12] I think Mr. Sandburg is quite right. Every child should be consecrated to the Lord, believed in and released to be who God has called him or her to be.

"A baby is God's opinion that the world should go on."

Regardless of how perfect or imperfect your child is according to the world's standards, you must continue to believe in him or her. When you falter in your courage, believe in the God who created your child and believe in the consecration you made.

In your motherhood journey there may be days, months or years that a "sword will pierce your own soul too," but that doesn't mean life should stop for you or your child. It doesn't mean you should give up and walk away. Charles Spurgeon, speaking of a mother, once said, "She never quite leaves her children at home, even when she doesn't take them along." [13] What an incredibly true statement! Once you've embarked on the journey of motherhood, there's no turning back. Long before Mary consecrated her child, she consecrated herself, and that was what she held fast to as she looked the future in the face. May the same be true of you.

Rewards of Consecration

PSALMS 127:3: *"Behold, children are a heritage from the Lord, the fruit of the womb is a reward." (NKJV)*

PSALMS 102:28: *"The children of Your servants will continue, and their descendants will be established before You." (NKJV)*

EXODUS 32:29: *"Consecrate yourselves today to the Lord, that He may bestow on you a blessing this day." (NKJV)*

ISAIAH 44:3: *"For I will pour water on him who is thirsty, and floods on the dry ground; I will pour My Spirit on your descendants, and My blessing on your offspring." (NKJV)*

PSALMS 128:3-6: *"Your wife shall be like a fruitful vine in the very heart of your house, your children like olive plants all around your table. Behold, thus shall the man be blessed who fears the Lord. The Lord bless you ... Yes, may you see your children's children." (NKJV)*

ISAIAH 65:23-24: *"They shall not labor in vain, nor bring forth children for trouble; for they shall be the descendants of the blessed of the Lord, and their offspring with them. It shall come to pass that before they call, I will answer; and while they are still speaking I will hear." (NKJV)*

HEBREWS 10:19-23: *"Therefore, brethren, having boldness to enter the Holiest by the blood of Jesus, by a new and living way which He consecrated for us, through the veil, that is, His flesh, and having a High Priest over the house of God, let us draw near with a true heart in full assurance of faith, having our hearts sprinkled from an evil conscience and our bodies washed with pure water. Let us hold fast the confession of our hope without wavering, for He who promised is faithful."*

LUKE 18:16: *"But Jesus called them to Him and said, 'Let the little children come to Me, and do not forbid them; for of such is the kingdom of God.'" (NKJV)*

PROVERBS 20:7: *"The righteous man walks in his integrity; his children are blessed after him." (NKJV)*

PROVERBS 17:6: *"Children's children are the crown of old men, and the glory of children is their father." (NKJV)*

NOTES

1   Genesis 17:12 NIV

2   *"And on the eighth day the flesh of his foreskin shall be circumcised. She shall then continue in the blood of her purification thirty-three days. She shall not touch any hallowed thing, nor come into the sanctuary until the days of her purification are fulfilled....When the days of her purification are fulfilled, whether for a son or a daughter, she shall bring to the priest a lamb of the first year as a burnt offering, and a young pigeon or a turtledove as a sin offering to the door of the tabernacle of meeting. Then he shall offer it before the Lord, and make atonement for her. And she shall be clean from the flow of her blood. This is the law for her who has borne a male or a female. And if she is not able to bring a lamb, then she may bring two turtledoves or two young pigeons – one as a burnt offering and the other as a sin offering. So the priest shall make atonement for her and she will be clean."* Leviticus 12:3-8

3   Exodus 13:2 NIV

4   Ps. 89:27-29 NIV

5   Dan. 9:24-27 NIV

6   Lk. 2:29-32 NIV

7   Mark 1:15 NIV

8   Lk 2:34,35 NIV

9   Eccl. 11:5 KJV

10 Ps. 126:6 KJV

11 Isa. 53:2 NIV

12 *A Mother Is to Cherish* (Nashville: Thomas Nelson Publishers, 1994), n.p.

13 Ibid.

Trust for Daily Provisions

After Jesus was born in Bethlehem in Judea, during the time of King Herod, Magi from the east came to Jerusalem and asked, "Where is the one who has been born king of the Jews? We saw his star in the east and have come to worship him." When King Herod heard this he was disturbed, and all Jerusalem with him. After they had heard the king, they went on their way, and the star they had seen in the east went ahead of them until it stopped over the place where the child was. When they saw the star, they were overjoyed. On coming to the house, they saw the child with his mother Mary, and they bowed down and worshipped him. Then they opened their treasures and presented him with gifts of gold and of incense and of myrrh. And having been warned in a dream not to go back to Herod, they returned to their country by another route. When they had gone, an angel of the Lord appeared to Joseph in a dream. "Get up," he said, "take the child and his mother and escape to Egypt. Stay there until I tell you, for Herod is going to search for the child to kill him." So he got up, took the child and his mother during the night and left for Egypt, where he stayed until the death of Herod. — Matthew 2:1-3, 9-15

The atmosphere in Jerusalem was tense. In mid-morning an entire entourage of magi from somewhere in the East came parading into the city and had just been seen leaving Herod's palace. Unexpected visitors in the city, especially those who came unannounced to his palace expecting an audience with him, tended to unnerve Herod, and when Herod wasn't happy, nobody was happy in Jerusalem. Speculation was running rampant and assumptions were being made that made everyone uncomfortable.

Where had these magi come from? Some said they appeared to be Arabian, others were sure that they talked like they were from Asia Minor, but most agreed that they looked like they were from somewhere in Persia. More importantly, where were they going? The word on the street was that Herod did give them an audience, but they obviously hadn't stayed long. Why, had he commissioned them to some task; had they warned him of some impending doom; what was it? What did these Gentile magi know that the average citizen of Jerusalem did not?

It was obvious to anyone who knew anything that Herod was declining in health and aging rapidly. Augustus was also advanced in years, and since the retirement of Tiberius, Rome had been without an experienced military commander. In fact, Phraates IV of Parthia was a very unpopular and aging king himself. The Persian Parthians did have leaders who had Jewish blood running through their veins. Could it be that these men from the East had a new king in view? Was it someone for Rome, for Persia, or perhaps for another nation?

From block to block speculation was increasing. The word on the streets that had supposedly come from someone, who knew someone, who knew someone among Herod's palace guards, was that they told Herod they were following a star and looking for "the one who has been born king of the Jews."[1] What an obvious, calculated insult to Herod! How did he take it? What would he do in response? Could he be bothered by their questions, or would he have the horses cinched up and the chariots ready to blaze a trail after the seemingly noncombatant entourage anytime soon?

Could it be that God was using a supernatural star to lead these astrologers out of their heathen land? Perhaps they had read Balaam's prophecy: "I see him, but not now; I behold him, but not near. A star will come out of Jacob; a scepter will rise out of Israel." [2] After all, in days past He had led His people out of Egypt by a pillar of cloud by day and a pillar of fire by night, why a star now? [3]

In addition to all the rumors, every knowledgeable Jew knew that Daniel's prophecy would soon come to pass, but what would Herod do if he realized it? What did he know? What did these magi know? Who were they looking for and where were they going?

Little did the populace of Jerusalem realize that by the time they were done talking about the entourage from the East, the magi would have traveled on to Bethlehem and departed again. Bethlehem was only six miles from Jerusalem, a relatively easy traveling distance for this gift-bearing group. They would be the first Gentiles to pay homage to the Christ child, but not the last. They were only the first among many who would bow their knee to Him.

*They would be the first Gentiles to pay homage
to the Christ child, but not the last.*

Jesus was a toddler now, busy about play and enjoying his surroundings. His curly brown hair and expressive brown eyes caused everyone who met him to laugh along with his contagious giggle no matter how great their current stress. His favorite thing to do was to toddle back and forth between Mary and Joseph and fall playfully into the security of their arms. Life was simple, but peaceful. These were days of not knowing what was coming next, and yet completely trusting in the Father.

Following the magi's visit in the early afternoon, it was naptime for the baby and Mary and Joseph lay down to rest as well. They were both in awe and wonder at what had just happened. They had been making ends meet there in Bethlehem, with Joseph's carpentry business afoot again, but the gifts the magi had brought to them could support them financially for at least two years.

As they rested, Joseph immediately fell into a deep sleep and the Lord appeared to him in a dream, saying, "Arise, take the young Child and His mother, flee to Egypt, and stay there until I bring you word: for Herod will seek the young Child to destroy Him." [4] Joseph rose up immediately and awakened Mary and told her what the Lord had spoken to him. *We must go tonight, Mary; pack quickly. I will get fodder for the donkey and prepare to load the travel cart.* Knowing that when the Lord spoke to Joseph through a dream, she could trust that the Lord was indeed speaking, Mary immediately arose and began to pack.

As she packed, she prayed, *Help me to know what to pack and what to leave, Lord. You will protect us, I know. Do watch over our precious child; he is dearer to me than life itself.* Feeling a need to remind the Lord of His promises, she continued, *The psalmist said, 'Praise be to the Lord, to God our Savior, who daily bears our burdens. Our God is a God who saves; from the Sovereign Lord comes escape from death.'* [5] *Let it be so, Father,* she prayed.

Praise soon filled her heart as she packed and Jesus napped on, *Thank You for Your bountiful provisions, the gifts to bring money and the dream to bring refuge. Your timing is amazing and Your care is abundant.*

As she bagged the last cooking pot and tin plate, little Jesus awakened with a smile and a knowing giggle of delight to see her so nearby. He reached for her and Joseph reached for his little tunic and wrapped him up in love and a nearby blanket and they closed their Bethlehem door and headed for Egypt. They headed out of town by dusk and were well on their way by nightfall.

This time, Mary would be able to find a place of refuge for her baby, but there was coming a day when there would be no provision for Him but a cross. The Gentile magi came with money that would provide temporary refuge, and gifts that symbolized His life and death as an offering to God. Although these Gentiles would be the first to proclaim Him as King of the Jews, there would be another Gentile, named Pilate, who would be the last to do so in this time period; and he would proclaim it through a placard on a cross.

Egypt, the land that had once represented bondage and oppression to Jews, was now a place of refuge and safety for Mary and her son. The very land in which her descendants had suffered under the heavy hand of ungodly Egyptian kings would now be a land of safety. Their stay in Egypt would be adequately financed by the unexpected gifts of the magi who did not know their God.

How sad that Herod, a Jewish king who should have known and understood the Old Testament prophecies, did not personally search for this new young king to properly honor Him. Rather, he sought to kill Him instead. How glorious that these Gentile magi did seek Him out, and honored Him. How strange and yet how wonderful that God's provision came to Mary and Joseph from unexpected people in unexpected ways.

Have there ever been times in your mothering that you were in great need of God's miraculous provision? Have there ever been times when you needed a place of refuge as well as food on the table?

God's provision comes in a variety of ways. It comes when we're watching and waiting, and it comes when we least expect it. It comes when we've worked hard to be a part of the provision and when we've done nothing to deserve it. God wants us to feel secure, but He loves to surprise us. Truly, He is a most wonderful provider.

God's provision comes in a variety of ways. It comes when we're watching and waiting, and it comes when we least expect it.

Marion was from western Canada. She and her husband had purchased a six-acre farm with the intention of subdividing and selling it in the future. He was developing his own business when he unexpectedly died, leaving Marion with little financial security for her and her children, ages two and four.

Four years after her husband's death, she met the Lord Jesus as her personal Savior and her heart began to burn with desire for Bible training and the mission field. In the eyes of most people, being a young widow and the mother of two and living on a limited budget would have been overwhelming obstacles. But not to Marion, to her they were simple challenges she needed to continually yield to her loving heavenly Father.

She was an energetic and intelligent woman, but how would she fulfill this new desire consuming her heart? Her friends wondered, her daughters trusted, and she listened to the Father's voice.

Her friends wondered, her daughters trusted,
and she listened to the Father's voice.

As a widow, Marion received $40 a month from the government for financial aid. She sold eggs, milk and fruit from the land to make ends meet. She also learned how to raise calves and have them butchered.

Several years later she even got a part-time job doing bookkeeping. She sewed and did her best to shop wisely at second-hand stores to clothe her daughters. The girls got a new pair of shoes twice each year for their growing feet and a new coat every two years.

After her salvation experience, Marion immediately began to tithe what little she had. Her butchered calves became her tithe for a season. She trusted God and His ability to provide, more than she trusted her own ability to budget. Her theme verse during this period in her life was "Trust in the Lord with all your heart and lean not on your own understanding; in all your ways acknowledge him, and he will make your paths straight". (Pro. 3:5,6)

She and her daughters prayed together every day for God to provide. Then with grateful hearts they thanked Him for His provision. Her oldest daughter recalls, "God always provided enough. We never went hungry. In fact, we [my sister and I] didn't realize we were 'poor' until we got older."

When Marion's daughters were ages 13 and 11, she was prompted by the Lord to sell the farm and move to the United States to attend Bible College and see what the Lord would do. Her plan was to stretch out her college education to seven years so that her youngest child could finish high school in the same location.

As an international college student, she was only permitted to work 20 hours a week. However, the sale of the property provided enough money on a monthly basis to pay their rent, her college fees and her daughters' school fees. This lasted four years before the new owner of the farm passed away and his heirs stopped payment on the land.

Now what would she do? She trusted the Lord and did her part, and He did His. Again, her theme song was "Trust in the Lord with all your heart and lean not on your own understanding." As she trusted, God did one little miracle after another. I don't know if America is an appropriate likeness to ancient Egypt, but I do know that God blessed this faithful mother and took care of her and her children in a foreign land.

One year after her return to her homeland, the farmland was turned back into her hands and she was able to resell it. Today she administrates a Christian overseas correspondence school for her local church. She also writes Bible curriculum for students who live in other nations and are hungry for sound doctrine and Bible teaching.

Her eldest daughter is married and she and her husband are leaders of evangelism in their local church. They have given her three beautiful grandchildren. Her youngest daughter is married and is a high school English teacher in Canada and spent several summers teaching English in overseas nations. A heart for God's people and for the nations reigns in both of their hearts.

Is this mother's dream being fulfilled? Was her trust in God to provide daily for her and her daughters worthy of her trust? Yes! Not only is she fulfilling her dream of reaching a mission field, her seed is multiplied and she is touching many through her writing as well as through her daughters' lives.

Like Mary, this mother was on a journey that would take her to a near-distant land. To succeed, she would need to be brave, trusting and wise. Her provisions for the journey would be minimal but adequate. Her seeds of trust have been multiplied many times over. God's daily provision has been abundant beyond anything she could ever imagine.

A wise man once said, "Do not carve your name on a tree or a wall, write it on the heart of a little child." [6] What you leave in your children will always be more important than what you leave to them. The deposit of faith that Marion and Mary left in their children was indelibly written on their hearts and affected their walks.

> *What you leave in your children will always be more important than what you leave to them.*

You may not be a widow and you may not have an insecure Eastern tyrant searching for your children with the intention of slaying them. However, we all need to trust the Lord at times for provision, both in our mothering and for our children.

Did you ever feel helpless when your child was being bullied or mocked by his or her peers? Did you ever shed a tear when your child forgot the notes in the middle of a music recital or missed the goal in the championship soccer match? Did you ever feel like spending more money than your budget would allow for the sake of a pair of shoes or jeans with a label on it? Did you ever wonder why God seems to bless some people more than others?

If you've done any of these things, maybe it's not an escape to Egypt you need. Maybe it's a respite in God's presence. What is my recommendation? Tie a knot in your emotional rope and hang on; God has a blessing for you on the other end.

It won't be long before you'll be pondering questions like these: Did you ever cry when you heard your daughter sing the national anthem at a basketball game? Did you ever wipe away a tear when your son testified in youth camp at the beginning of the week rather than the end? Did you ever silently rejoice when your child gave all of his or her hard-earned money to a poor family at Christmas? Did you ever maintain your composure on the outside but shout on the inside, *Yes! That's my kid!* Did you ever just stop and thank God for His marvelous, miraculous, amazing daily provisions?

Promises of Provision

PHILIPPIANS 4:19: *"And my God shall supply all your need according to His riches in glory by Christ Jesus." (NKJV)*

PSALMS 37:4,5: *"Delight yourself also in the Lord, and He shall give you the desires of your heart. Commit your way to the Lord, trust also in Him, and He shall bring it to pass." (NKJV)*

PSALMS 2:12: *"Blessed are those who put their trust in Him." (NKJV)*

DEUTERONOMY 2:7: *"For the Lord your God has blessed you in all that you have done;…your God has been with you; you have not lacked a thing." (NASB)*

DEUTERONOMY 8:7-9: *"For the Lord your God is bringing you into a good land, a land of brooks of water, of fountains and springs, flowing forth in valleys and hills; …a land where you will eat food without scarcity, in which you will not lack anything." (NASB)*

I THESSALONIANS 4:9-12: *"But concerning brotherly love you have no need that I should write to you, for you yourselves are taught by God to love one another; and indeed you do so toward all the brethren who are in all Macedonia. But we urge you, brethren, that you increase more and more; that you also aspire to lead a quiet life to mind your own business, and to work with your own hands, as we commanded you, that you may walk properly toward those who are outside, and that you may lack nothing." (NASB)*

PROVERBS 11:25: *"The generous man will be prosperous, and he who waters will himself be watered." (NASB)*

PSALMS 34:8: *"Oh, taste and see that the Lord is good; blessed is the man who trusts in Him!" (NKJV)*

PSALMS 34:10: *"Those who seek the Lord shall not lack any good thing." (NKJV)*

PSALMS 84:11-12: *"For the Lord God is a sun and shield; the Lord will give grace and glory; no good thing will He withhold from those who walk uprightly; O Lord of hosts, blessed is the man who trusts in You!" (NKJV)*

PSALMS 85:12: *"Yes, the Lord will give what is good; and our land will yield its increase." (NKJV)*

NOTES

1   *"The Star of Bethlehem has been called many things by many people; a comet, a conjunction of palets, a supernova, a miracle, a myth.... Michael R. Molnar, an astronomer and physicist and former teacher at Rutgers University, proposes that the star was the planet Jupiter, seen in the constellation Aries the Ram.... 'Jupiter was considered to be the regal star or regal planet,' Molnar said in an interview. Thus the two events on the same day would have been looked upon by the wise men, or magi, who were astrologers, as strong portents of the birth of a great king. The fact that Jupiter appeared in Aries, in the east, had further significance, Molnar said, as Aries was considered the symbol of Judea....I found that the Magi practiced what historians call Greek astrology, which is the basis for modern Western astrology. Greek astrology partnered very closely with Stoic philosophy—fate ruled the world. And astrologers professed that they could predict fate by monitoring planetary positions.'"* Henry Fountain, New York Times News Service, *The Road to Bethlehem,* The Oregonian, A8, December 24, 1999, [interview of Michael R. Molnar, by Henry Fountain of New York Times News Service, quotes in article taken from *The Star of Behlehem, The Legacy of the Magi,* by Michael R. Molnar, Source: Rutgers University Press].

2   Numbers 24:17 NIV

3   See Exodus 13:21

4   Mt. 2:13 NIV

5   Ps. 68:19,20 NIV

6   Some attribute this quote to Charles Spurgeon, source unknown.

A Mother's Formative Influence

When Joseph and Mary had done everything required by the Law of the Lord, they returned to Galilee to their own town of Nazareth. And the child grew and became strong; he was filled with wisdom, and the grace of God was upon him. — *Luke 2:39,40*

Mary could feel Jesus' little hands playing with her hair, brushing it back from her face to see if she was awake yet. She opened her sleepy eyes to see his big brown eyes getting closer to her as if to investigate who she really was in the early morning dimly lit room. *"Mommy, mommy,"* he whispered, patting her face gently, knowing that in the early morning before the household door was open to the outside world, he must be very quiet.

Next to her on the other side she could hear Joseph breathing deeply. She quietly sat up and nestled little Jesus in her arms, putting one finger over her mouth as if to say to him to *'please, be quiet for just one more moment.'* He dutifully stepped back off of his little mat and she rolled it up quietly placing it in the corner of the room. She reached for the tunics and pulled his on first and then hers. Then she swept him up in her arms, grabbed a bag of figs and headed out the door. Climbing the hillside one small step at a time, they went to their favorite morning place of prayer just above their home.

It was so good to be back in Nazareth and back to her favorite hillside place of prayer. Jesus, four years old now, loved to go there with her in the early morning. When he was just two and three, he would imitate her, folding his hands and speaking his childlike prayers to his heavenly Father. Now that he was four, sometimes he would repeat what she had taught him to pray, and other times he would pray out-loud on his own about needs for neighbors and friends that he had either observed himself or that he had heard Mary and Joseph speaking about. The depth of his simple prayers never ceased to amaze her.

On this hillside it was easy for her to recall when Gabriel came to her. She knew now that it was a sovereign spirit of faith in her that had responded to him, knowing that she really had no idea what she was getting herself into when she responded with *"I am your servant. Let it be to me as you have said."* Although she did not ever regret her response, at times she felt quite overwhelmed by the responsibility set before her. This morning was one of those mornings.

The greater percentage of her parenting with young Jesus was filled with laughter, simple instruction, and many opportunities to say *"yes"* to his childlike requests. When he was one and two it seemed there were more yes's than no's, and yet the no's were painful for both of them. When she looked at him and slowly, but firmly said *"noooo,"* his lower lip would protrude and his eyes would fill with tears, looking up at her realizing he had disappointed her. Then he would rub his eyes and reach up to her to receive her forgiveness and approval. She used more 'distract and divert' tactics than anything else, because saying *"no"* to God's son somehow seemed backward, even though He had put him in her trust, as fully-man though fully-God.

Reflecting back on the ones and twos, she was thankful for the threes and fours. Actually, it had all been fun, if she were completely honest, but these were days of more yes's than no's. As the sun peaked over the horizon, she and Jesus applauded and lifted their hands and said together, *"Thank You Lord; we praise You for the sunrise!"* He smiled at her and she at him, then they hugged and giggled and rolled to the ground. Then they sat back up, both folding their hands and bowing their heads, and taking turns, began to pray. This was a morning ritual that they both enjoyed. Sometimes he would look at her quizzically and ask her a question like, *"What makes the sunrise, Mommy?"* and *"Why don't butterflies sing like birds do?"*

After praying together for awhile and answering a question or two, it wouldn't be long before something on this special little hillside would distract him and he would walk or run away to investigate. This morning it was a small white butterfly, as it flitted from flower to flower nearby. While Jesus chased the butterfly, she began to focus personally on Jehovah. She knew he wouldn't go far, he was well aware of the allowable distance he could be from her. His usual early morning game was to go a little ways off and then run back to her arms with a big hug and kiss. Then he would sit and fold his hands and pray two or three sentences and then wander off again. Sometimes, to her surprise, he would pray for four or five minutes at a time. He would repeat this delightful routine of praying, running, and hugging over and over, until it was time to return and do their morning chores.

As she watched him run and play, the responsibility of motherhood in these formative years, as delightful as they were, began to overwhelm her thoughts. *You really did it, Father,* she prayed. *You really placed the life of this supernatural, yet completely natural and delightful, child in my arms. My heart is overwhelmed. "I call on you, O God, for you will answer me; give ear to me and hear my prayer."* [1]

She continued her request, *Lord, as Isaiah of old said, please give me "an instructed tongue." [2] Waken me morning by morning; waken my ear to listen like one being taught. Sovereign Lord, who "wakens my ear to listen, open my ears that I might know what to say and what to do." [3] Make me a mother who can discern the questions of His spirit and the intents of His heart. Cause me to imprint on His spirit that which You have destined."*

Now with early morning questions of her own, *"Where do I begin? You are so amazing and He is so precious! Oh, is that where I begin—with 'amazing' and 'precious?' Yes, Lord, I'll begin there. I'll enjoy the precious-*

ness of this season and stand in amazement of the wonder of it all. Thank You, Lord for Your encouragement." Looking at Jesus, now seeing him run back to her to leap into her arms for another delightful hug and big kiss on the cheek, with a tear of joy in her eye, she whispered to heaven, *"Thank You, Father. I delight to do Your will."* Taking him by the hand, together they began to run down the hill welcoming the day with giggles of delight.

Every good Jewish home was the center of religious training in the early years of a young boy's life. But Mary wanted more for Jesus than the simple memorization of Scripture reading and writing. Solomon of old had said, "The fear of the Lord is the beginning of knowledge...Listen, my son, to your father's instruction and do not forsake your mother's teaching" (Prov. 1:7,8, NIV). Mary knew that she, along with Joseph, was responsible to impart the truths of God's word to Jesus in his early years. Where to begin must have been a challenge. What should she emphasize; how should she go about it; where should she start? Where would you begin with God's son?

Mary must have felt somewhat overwhelmed by the responsibility set before her. She knew when Gabriel, God's messenger, came to her that he was asking something big of her. She knew that her trust in the Father's guidance would have to deepen in her spirit. She also knew that she needed God's wisdom to guide her day by day, even moment by moment, requiring of her a surrendered and listening ear.

Have you ever looked at your child and felt overwhelmed at the obvious responsibility before you? Have you ever assessed how many of your own mother's qualities you do and do not personify, and then wondered how many of your own qualities your child will show? Have you ever pondered the indelible, inerasable marking that you make on your child's life every day?

I can remember the first parent-teacher conference my husband and I had with one of our children's first teachers. She complimented us on the child. (Attention all mothers! That's just the warm-up.) Then as she continued to discuss our child's classroom habits, after each assessment she contemplatively said, "And I don't know why your child does that." Each time she made that statement, my husband and I took turns looking at each other with blameshifting eyes that humorously said, "That's you! You're the reason for that one!"

The session was brief, but it seemed like a 48-hour emotional undressing, layer by layer. We walked out of that parent-teacher conference convinced that parenting was going to give us much more *exposure* than we ever imagined. Although this teacher never openly pointed a finger at us and said, "You are the cause," we both knew that our little charge was definitely affected by us, for better or worse. What an unexpected and rude awakening! It was, in fact, not only humbling, it was rather frightening.

Parenting was going to give us much more
EXPOSURE than we ever imagined.

I have a wonderful friend who once pastored alongside her husband in the mid-west; today they are pastor-teachers in a Bible college setting. They are both vibrant, godly people who have done their best to serve the Lord together for many years.

When they were a young couple pastoring their first church and their bouncing, blond-haired, blue-eyed baby boy came along, they couldn't have been happier. They already had a beautiful brown-haired, brown-eyed girl just a few years older; all was well and peaceful within their world. But they soon discovered that this little fellow definitely had a mind of his own; in fact, 'strong-willed' seemed to be a mild term for him.

When he was four years old, he had a set of Bible storybooks at home from which both of his parents read to him on a regular basis. During one phase of this season, he became especially intrigued with the story in the book of Daniel about the three Hebrew children who were thrown into the fiery furnace. At the same time he was also very interested in the concept of hell and how people could end up there.

He regularly attended children's church on Sunday mornings with all the other children. Of course, since he was the associate pastor's son, he had no real options other than this. He was energetic, curious by nature and usually somewhat mischievous during children's church. One day he was particularly disruptive. His blond hair and sparkling blue eyes were not going to help him escape discipline this day. The teachers collectively decided to place him on a chair in the corner, facing the wall. As soon as they resumed teaching, the little tyke stood up on his chair and began to yell at the teachers in front of the whole group, "You are all going to burn in hell for putting me in this corner!"

For the rest of the year, on Sundays he sat with his mother on the front row of church. His "children's church" was near her side in the "big people's" church service.

While administrating a summertime vacation Bible school two years later, this young mother once again came to grips with the extremes to which her six-year-old would go. She was extremely busy with all of the details of her job description for the week: coordinating teachers, class locations, crafts, refreshments and a variety of other details.

One day, one of her son's teachers, looking rather sheepish and embarrassed, came to her and said, "I'm sure this probably isn't true, but your son has just requested special prayer for you and your husband. He says he's unable to go to sleep at night because you are up until two in the morning every night screaming at each other fighting." Then the teacher looked at her and said, "Is there a problem that we need to know about? Can we help in any way?"

The son's "prayer request" was a lie, and it put his mother and his teacher in the middle of a memorable, but embarrassing, moment. Did this young mother need to impart the importance of truth, regardless of what humorous reactions lies would get, to her son? Yes, she did. Did she need the ability to assess a situation and wait for the suitable time to address it? Most definitely. Did her future hold some challenges with this bright, quick-witted child? Yes, it did. Did she need a sense of humor, as well as the wisdom of God to raise him? Absolutely.

Today, this son is a fine young married man with two sons of his own. He's truthful, industrious for the Lord, and has a great relationship with his parents. He only has accolades for them, as they do for him. There are no more lies about his parent's marriage or false predictions about children's church teachers burning in hell in his mouth. This mother and son made it through, because she, like Mary, held on to the hope that was within her and took the time to mold and influence him for Christ in his formative years.

Jesus' education, under Mary's tutelage, would have begun at the age of three with much memorization of Scripture. Between the ages of five and ten he would have learned to read and write and study the Scripture.

The household duties of the Jewish mother included "grinding flour, cooking, laundry, making beds, and spinning wool. She was also supposed to maintain an attractive appearance for her husband. The husband was required to provide her with food and clothing, maintain regular sexual relations, provide for the children, and was forbidden to strike her. The woman's influence in the family was considered greater than the man's." [4]

Needless to say, Mary had her work cut out for her. As a mother, she had specific responsibilities outlined by her culture, including the responsibility to impart a solid upbringing and knowledge of the Scriptures to her children. I have a suspicion that Mary did it with joy as well.

Even though in our contemporary culture we may not find ourselves grinding flour or spinning wool apart from specific nutritional desires or the sheer novelty of it, we do still have a responsibility to impart the Word of God and Spirit of Christ to our children. It is through imparting Christ that security, emotional stability and healthy citizenry will grow in our children.

It is through imparting Christ that security, emotional stability and healthy citizenry will grow in our children.

Healing evangelist Kathryn Kuhlman once said, "I can never remember, as a child, having my mother show me any affection. Never. Mama was a perfect disciplinarian. But she never once told me she was proud of me or that I did well. Never once. It was Papa who gave me the love and affection." [5] Her biographer wrote:

> After Kathryn became famous, she used to get on the phone at night and call her mother back in Concordia, talking for hours at a time. According to the telephone operator, Kathryn was constantly trying to prove to her mother that she had succeeded. "She would giggle and giggle," the former operator told me, "and of course we'd sit there listening and giggle too. Then she would tell her mother all she had gotten: 'Mama, I've got the biggest Christmas tree in the city. It's sooooo tall, and has more than 5,000 lights on it.' She would talk about the size of the offering at her miracle services as if she was trying to convince her mother that she was a success." [6]

What a sad narrative. I'm sure that Kathryn's mother loved her. But her inability to impart that love to her daughter early in her life left Kathryn in need of constant reassurance of her acceptance. Sadly, it also left her insecurity exposed to prying eyes and listening ears.

Corrie Ten Boom, well-known speaker and heroine of the anti-Nazi underground, had a different experience with her mother. She was incredibly attentive to Corrie and to those who were less fortunate, continually creating 'a very special occasion' for them all. She generously gave to others while simultaneously mentoring her daughter in kindness and sensitivity to the needs of those less fortunate.

Mama could have coffee on the stove and a cake in the oven as fast as most people could say "best wishes." And since she knew almost everyone in Harlem, especially the poor, sick and neglected, there was almost no day in the year that was not for somebody, as she would say with eyes shining, "a very special occasion!"[7]

I wonder if it was through this impartation that Corrie received the grace and kindness to give to the poor, sick, neglected, and even to the undeserving later in life. She tells in the end of her autobiography:

It was at a church service in Munich that I saw him, the former SS man who had stood guard at the shower room door in the processing center at Ravensbruck. He was the first of our actual jailers that I had seen since that time. And suddenly it was all there—the room full of mocking men, the heaps of clothing, Betsie's pain-blanched face.

He came up to me as the church was emptying, beaming and bowing. "How grateful I am for your message, Fraulein," he said. "To think that, as you say, He has washed my sins away!"

His hand was thrust out to shake mine. And I, who had preached so often to the people in Bloemendaal the need to forgive, kept my hand at my side.

Even as the angry, vengeful thoughts boiled through me, I saw the sin of them. Jesus Christ had died for this man; was I going to ask for more? *Lord Jesus, I prayed, forgive me and help me to forgive him.*

I tried to smile, I struggled to raise my hand. I could not. I felt nothing, not the slightest spark of warmth or charity. And so again I breathed a silent prayer. *Jesus, I cannot forgive him. Give me Your forgiveness.*

As I took his hand the most incredible thing happened. From my shoulder along my arm and through my hand a current seemed to pass from me to him, while into my heart sprang a love for this stranger that almost overwhelmed me.

And so I discovered that it is not on our forgiveness any more than on our goodness that the world's healing hinges, but on His. When He tells us to love our enemies, He gives, along with the command, the love itself. [8]

Yes, it was both Christ's forgiveness and the compassion of Corrie's mother for the poor, sick and neglected that had graced her own life with supernatural love for this enemy. The SS officer had left an indelible mark on Corrie's soul, not one that was easily forgiven. But the more deeply engraved mark was that of her mother's life example and that of the Lord Jesus Christ.

This was a pivotal point in her life, as she reached out to Christ, He reached back to her. In an instant a firebrand touched her heart, healed her wounds and imparted love itself. From this time on, she was free to impart that same grace, not only to the wounded she identified with, but also to the wounded beyond her natural ability to love whom Christ died for as well.

As she reached out to Christ, He reached back to her.

There are so many unsung heroines among the long list of mothers through the ages. I must tell you of one more who imparted much to her daughter. This mother's name was Drana Bojaxhiu. She came from a large, well-established family in Prizren, Albania. She was known to be gentle, engaging, generous and full of compassion toward the poor.

She became a widow and was left with three children to raise. Their ages were fifteen, eleven and eight. To support the family after the death of her husband, she embroidered and made bridal dresses and costumes for various festivals.

No matter how little she had, she always had something to give to the poor. Her youngest daughter, Agnes, said, "Never did anyone go away empty-handed. Every day at the table something was left for the poor. The first time, I asked my mother, 'Who are they?' She replied: 'Some are relatives; the others are our own people.' When I grew up I understood that these were the poor people who had nothing, but whom my mother fed." [9]

Drana often told her children, "When you do good, do it as if you were casting a stone into the depth of the sea."

Agnes says of her family memories, "Ours was a happy family, full of joy, of love, and of happy children." [10]

Agnes Bojaxhiu is known to most today, as Mother Teresa, who spent many years of her life in India. She opened several places of refuge for the dying, especially those with leprosy. She also started many orphanages for abandoned children and orphans. She trained others to care for the poor, and she affected a generation with the love of Christ. It was commonly know that at 85 years of age, she slept only three to four hours a night and prayed five hours a day.

When seeking the Lord concerning her call to the mission field as a young woman, she said that she could hear in her heart her mother's words: "When you take on a task, do it willingly; otherwise, do not accept it." [11]

Yes, her mother's spirit and her words would ring in Agnes's ears for many years to come. That impartation would help carry her into the presence of the poor, diseased and dying; earthly kings and presidents; and ultimately the King of kings.

Whether you feed the poor, make tea for your neighbors or give grace to an enemy, know that your children are watching and being mentored by your actions. They will receive more from your example than you'll probably ever fully realize. But it will be obvious one day when you take a good long look at your grandchildren. Much of what we impart to our children will be passed on to another generation, for better or for worse.

*Much of what we impart to our children will be passed
on to another generation, for better or for worse.*

Don't be afraid; remember the promise: "He gently leads those that have young" (Isa. 40:11). So cling to His leading and watch "the child grow and become strong; filled with wisdom, and the grace of God" (Lk. 2:40).

Training and Instruction—
Partnering with the Lord

PROVERBS 22:6: *"Train up a child in the way he should go, even when he is old he will not depart from it." (NASB)*

PROVERBS 1:2-4: *"To know wisdom and instruction, to discern the sayings of understanding, to receive instruction in wise behavior, righteousness, justice and equity; to give prudence to the naïve, to the youth knowledge and discretion." (NASB)*

PROVERBS 1:8,9: *"Hear, my son, your father's instruction and do not forsake your mother's teaching; indeed, they are a graceful wreath to your head and ornaments about your neck."*

PROVERBS 4:13: *"Take hold of instruction; do not let go. Guard her, for she is your life." (NASB)*

PROVERBS 4:20-27: *"My son, give attention to my words; incline your ear to my sayings. Do not let them depart from your sight; keep them in the midst of your heart. For they are life to those who find them and health to all their body. Watch over your heart with all diligence, for from it flow the springs of life. Put away from you a deceitful mouth and put devious speech far from you. Let your eyes look directly ahead and let your gaze be fixed straight in front of you. Watch the path of your feet and all your ways will be established. Do not turn to the right nor to the left; turn your foot from evil."*

PROVERBS 6:20-23: *"My son, observe the commandment of your father and do not forsake the teaching of your mother; bind them continually on your heart; tie them around your neck. When you walk about, they will guide you; when you sleep, they will watch over you; and when you awake, they will talk to you. For the commandment is a lamp and the teaching is light; and reproofs for discipline are the way of life."(NASB)*

PROVERBS 7:1-4: *"My son, keep my words and treasure my commandments and live, and my teaching as the apple of your eye. Bind them on your fingers; write them on the tablet of your heart. Say to wisdom, 'You are my sister,' and call understanding your intimate friend." (NASB)*

EPHESIANS 6:4: *"Do not provoke your children to anger, but bring them up in the discipline and instruction of the Lord." (NASB)*

NOTES

1   Ps. 17:6 NIV

2   Isa. 50:4 NIV

3   Isa.50:5 NIV

4   Everett Ferguson, *Backgrounds of Early Christianity*, (Grand Rapids, Michigan: William B. Eerdmans, 1993), p. 71.

5   Jamie Buckingham, *Daughter of Destiny, Kathryn Kuhlman...Her Story*, (Plainfield, N.J.: Logos International, 1976), p. 15.

6   Ibid., p. 16

7   Corrie Ten Boom, *The Hiding Place*, (New York: Bantam Books, 1971), p. 6.

8   Ibid. p. 238

9   Lush Gjergji, *Mother Teresa: Her Life, Her Works*, (New York: New City Press, 1991), p. 15.

10 Ibid., p. 16.

11 Ibid., p. 12.

The Stages of Release

Releasing into Adolescence

Every year his parents went to Jerusalem for the Feast of the Passover. When he was twelve years old, they went up to the Feast, according to the custom. After the Feast was over, while his parents were returning home, the boy Jesus stayed behind in Jerusalem, but they were unaware of it. Thinking he was in their company, they traveled on for a day. Then they began looking for him among their relatives and friends. When they did not find him, they went back to Jerusalem to look for him. After three days they found him in the temple courts, sitting among the teachers, listening to them and asking them questions. Everyone who heard him was amazed at his understanding and his answers. When his parents saw him, they were astonished. His mother said to him, "Son, why have you treated us like this? Your father and I have been anxiously searching for you." "Why were you searching for me?" he asked. "Didn't you know I had to be in my Father's house?" But they did not understand what he was saying to them. Then he went down to Nazareth with them and was obedient to them. But his mother treasured all these things in her heart." — Luke 2:41-51

You could cut the tension in the air with a knife; their firstborn son was gone! Had he run away? If so, why? Had he been kidnapped? If so, why and by whom? Where was he? The city was large in size and population, but even more so during festival time.[1] How would they find him among nearly half a million people in over 300 acres of land?

Mary quickly made arrangements with other traveling companions in the caravan to take her other children home with them while she and Joseph headed back to Jerusalem to find Jesus. Joseph was sweating profusely and Mary was too. They both had feverishly been up and down the caravan of travelers asking if anyone had seen their son. Terror struck their hearts when they discovered that no one had seen him.

The tension, the hurry, the fear was overwhelming; they had already been out of the city one day without realizing his absence and it would take nearly another day to get back into the city. They walked as fast as their legs would carry them. Mary had a sharp pain in her right side from walking so fast and felt as if she would faint, but there was no time for fainting now, they must hurry back into the city before the sun began to set in the sky.

What if they couldn't find him? Where would he be—near the Pool of Bethesda, the Antonia Fortress, the Lower City, or the Upper City? Where should they look first? Would he be on a market street, in an unknown residential neighborhood, or on the palace steps? How would he ever hear them calling his name in the midst of the noisy sellers and bargaining buyers? What if he was harmed? What if he was lost to them forever?

As they quickened their pace, Mary's thoughts became verbal intercessions. *Oh Father, he's gone! You entrusted him into our care and he's gone! How could we be so careless? How could he be so mindless? He knows that Jerusalem's streets are not always safe during feast time. Why didn't he stay close to us like he knew to do? When he was small he would always hold tightly to my hand or stay within my view, but not anymore.*

Her petitions became frustrated venting. *I know that he is now an official son of the Law, but he's still my boy. I know he's older, but there are so many people who might do him harm! He knows better than to do this. How could he not be more careful?*

Her venting became presumptuous reminders to a heavenly Father who always had him within view and knew him better than she did. *He's so innocent great Jehovah, so unprepared for the real world. He's so inquisitive and trusting of people who might do him harm.* The cycle of fruitless venting returned to genuine petition, *Oh Father, please protect him; please watch over him. Please lead and guide our steps to him. My trust is in You.*

Coming upon the sounds of the city in late afternoon, fear blanketed in determination entered her heart. Joseph took her by the hand and they headed into the lower city, passed the Pool of Siloam, with their eyes canvassing the crowd. Next, they headed toward the business sector where the population intensified. There were people everywhere, *how would they find him?* They both began to yell out his name with intensity, barely being able to be heard over the din of the noisy sellers and festival bargainers. People hardly noticed as they shouted his name in despair.

Nearing nightfall now, they began to ask people if they had seen him, describing him to those who cared to listen. Sadly, most Jewish boys his age fit the same description. People were suggesting several different directions for them to go based on a boy that fit the description they gave. *Would they ever find him?*

Shops were closing up for the night and people were disappearing into inns to sleep for the night. Others were simply wrapping themselves in their outer tunics and sleeping on the streets, shushing them as they persisted in their calling and question asking. Finally, late into the night, they slumped against the wall that was one among many on market row and slept for the remaining night hours. All Mary could mutter was, *"Oh God, Who never slumbers nor sleeps, please keep a watchful eye on my beloved son. Protect him from the dangers of the night in this city. Please help our eyes to see him in the morning."*

By early morning, their stomachs growled from hunger and their mouths thirsted for drink, but their hearts remained more dissatisfied than any physical yearning they had. As the shops began to open and the pedlars began to pedal their wares, they scanned the people on the street and saw no one they had not seen the night before. They walked up and down the narrow streets, describing their son and asking nearly everyone they saw if they had seen him. They walked for hours, looking and praying. As the crowd and noise began to increase once again with the festival atmosphere, they began to shout out his name down dark alleyways and from the top of narrow stairways.

With desperation in their hearts they headed toward the Temple. Working their way through the mass of people slowly, they were hardly able to see more than three people ahead of them at a time. But they were determined to get to the Temple steps where they could perhaps get above the crowd and see into it. Then suddenly they saw him! He was sitting on the steps of the Temple dialoguing with the priests. *Why hadn't they thought of this earlier?* The priests always dialogued with passersby and eager young students during Feast Days. There he was, speaking with them as if he was the priest and they were the newly inducted Sons of the Law. They all seemed to be truly meditating on what he was saying to them.

Mary could not contain herself. With perspiration beading her brow and tears streaming down her face, she ran to him and threw her arms around him. *"Jesus, Jesus,"* she cried as she embraced him and then clasped her hands onto his face and looked him in the eyes as if to say, *'Are you alright?'* But before she could think she said, *"Young man, why have you done this to us? Your father and I have been half out of our minds looking for you."* [2]

He said, *"Why were you looking for me? Didn't know that I had to be here, dealing with the things of my Father?"*[3] Mary and Joseph felt confused. *What did he say—"…the things of his Father?"* They stepped back. They were speechless. Mary could feel the sword of Simeon penetrating her heart; everything was in slow motion. A new release in her motherhood journey had just taken place, and she did not know how to respond. She looked at him again, and without saying a word, she embraced him once again and turned him toward the street leading home to Nazareth.

As they walked the streets out of Jerusalem heading towards home, all three were in silent wonder at what had occurred on the Temple steps. The silence was not of frustration or disappointment; it was one of wonder and meditation. Mary pondered in her heart the words that Jesus had spoken to her, as did Joseph as well.

Have you ever felt as if your teenagers were just a step ahead of where you wanted them to be in their social independence? Have you ever thought they were in one place and then discovered they were in another? Have you ever wondered about the company they were keeping or if they were wise enough to realize when they were in danger? Sensing their transition from childhood to adulthood, have you ever rebuked them and then wondered if you handled the situation in the right way? Have you ever gone out of your way to make a celebration special for them only to discover their focus was elsewhere?

All of these questions and more must have gone through Mary's mind that day. Nazareth was approximately 70 miles from Jerusalem, and it was not uncommon for large numbers of families to travel together to and from the feasts.[4] It was also not uncommon for the women and small children, who traveled more slowly, to begin the journey home before the men, who would catch up to them by evening and set up camp for the night.

It's easy to understand how Jesus wasn't missed immediately. The reference to three days in this passage of Scripture probably refers to a day's journey away from Jerusalem, a day's journey back and a day of searching for Him in the city. Obviously, as soon as they realized Jesus was not with either of them, they returned to the city to search for Him.

Although all Jewish men within a certain radius of Jerusalem were required to attend the feasts, the women were not. However, Mary made a special effort to attend. This was a special year, the year that Jesus would become a son of the Law. Little did Mary know that for her, this trip would bring about the second stage of release of her firstborn son.

The Temple was not just a center for prayer, consecration and sacrifice; it was also a place for teaching. It was customary for the Sanhedrin to meet in public in the Temple court to discuss religious and theological questions. The Jewish teachers enjoyed conducting classes during feast times in the Temple courts.

Asking questions was a common mode of learning. In fact, the rabbis enjoyed being asked questions, not only to instruct, but also to show off their great knowledge. The only stipulation to the questions was that they be intelligent and thought provoking.

The passage of Scripture in Luke 2:47 indicates that Jesus' questions and responses were indeed intelligent and perceptive. The passage actually says that teachers were "amazed at his understanding and his answers." Although Jesus didn't perform any miracles here, the Greek text indicates that the teachers knew they were in the presence of a young man who was more than just a brilliant young student. They recognized the wisdom of God resting on Him. Luke had already noted in verse 40 that the grace of God was upon Jesus; this must have been apparent to His teachers in this setting as well.

Have you ever been amazed at insightful statements and perceptions made by your young teenagers? Has it ever seemed to you that one minute they act immature and the next minute they make some profound statement that goes over your head?

I can remember more than once being amazed by my teens when they shared with me a word of counsel they had given to a friend. The thoughts were beyond their years of understanding. I can also remember being amazed at how my son could administrate a party and the clean-up crew afterward as well; and I always marveled at his ability to work and program all the electronic gadgets around the house.

I can also recall the first time I heard my teen daughter practicing a piano piece that went beyond my own skills, and memorizing and reciting the book of Proverbs in its entirety. I could go on and on with examples, but I won't. As we all know, the wonder of a mother's memories is entertaining to her children but boring to most! I'm sure your teens have demonstrated certain perceptions and talents that have amazed you as well.

When Mary and Joseph found Jesus in the Temple, Mary spoke to Him as though he were a child. Any mother of a child in middle school knows this is a big mistake. Mary actually rebuked him for what she considered to be insensitivity on his part. In so many words, she told him, "You have acted like a child." Her joy in finding him was eclipsed by the frustration and anxiety she had experienced.

The commandment to honor one's father and mother was regarded by the Jews as one of the most important of all the laws. Children who were not yet considered to be adults were to express this honor, in part, by their obedience to their parents. It is here that Mary met with her second release. She spoke to Jesus as though he was a child, even though he had just become a recognized adult in the Jewish community. From him she received a gentle but firm and surprising response. When Mary said, "Your father and I...," Jesus gently and precisely responded by taking the title of father from Joseph and giving it to God.

History doesn't tell us if Jesus was aware of his deity prior to this. However, from this point on, he obviously knew who his Father was. His deity was now a spoken revelation to him and his mother, even though he may not have known all that it entailed at this point. Although Scripture says that Mary and Joseph did not understand what Jesus was saying, I'm sure they took it to heart and pondered it in the days following.

History doesn't tell us if Jesus was aware of his deity prior to this. However, from this point on, he obviously knew who his Father was.

If you have teens in your household, what have you been pondering lately? Are the rules and regulations of your household clear or do they change from day to day? Do you speak to your teen in the same manner in which you spoke to him or her in childhood days? Do you find yourself making a transition from instant-obedience-without-question to "come now, let us reason together?" [5] Has your style of discipline become a confusing issue for both you and your teen?

I can remember when a wise 'Elizabeth' said to me in one of my moments of frustration and questioning: "You have to discern between true rebellion and the 'little man' inside." She continued to explain to me that, especially with a son, a mother is the first woman he practices his leadership skills on. What a revelation!

You must discern between immaturity and disobedience, between "practice" and rebellion, in those moments of seemingly needed discipline. Granted, it's a precarious tightrope to walk. But if we assume that every disagreement is willful disrespect or disregard for our leadership as a parent, we may be missing the mark, especially with our sons.

You must discern between immaturity and disobedience, between "practice" and rebellion, in those moments of seemingly needed discipline.

There is a delicate balance of release in the teen years. Some parents hold on so tightly that their teens rebel against the parents' authority and guidance. They feel smothered and unable to grow, so they break away. Other parents let go of their teens to such an extreme that the teens feel unloved and bereft of genuine care. They feel lost in a maze in which they have no sense of mature guidance. They want direction but have been left to discover it for themselves.

Most of us are somewhere in between these two extremes, and it still feels precarious at times. Even though the events and moods in a teen's life can vary as much as the hairs on their heads, doing your best to enjoy the parenting adventure at every stage of the your child's life will only benefit your posture in this new season of release. Learn to ride the emotional ups and downs with grace and compassion rather than reaction and resentment.

Learn to ride the emotional ups and downs with grace and compassion rather than reaction and resentment.

There is no specific or set pattern for parenting your teens. Each child is an individual and has a specific blueprint for each season of his or her growth. But we can take a cue of how to release them into this season with confidence from Mary. Notice that after Jesus and she had this encounter, she did not rebuke him further, and he came home and served her as the firstborn son for the next eighteen years of his life. Most biblical scholars refer to these as the "silent years" of his life, as we have no records of any specific life events during this season.

I'm sure that in this instance Mary must have been startled by his response. I'm sure that she must have felt a bit confused, perhaps frustrated and resentful that he had not been more responsible and had caused such fear in her heart. Yet she obviously quickly postured herself to receive revelation from the Father for this moment in her life. She did not speak hastily to him again and pondered carefully what he had said.

You will also be amazed at how God will cover you and your role as a parent, even when you are wrong or do not display the attitude He would desire from you. God will always stand by you in your parental position, unless you are abusing it. He has ordained it to be so. However, discernment is important. For God warns parents: "Do not exasperate your children; instead bring them up in the training and instruction of the Lord" (Eph. 6:4).

Just as, I am sure, Mary felt anxiety about releasing her obviously strong-minded, perceptive young teen at this season, there was another mother in history who must have had similar emotions about releasing her young teen. She was the mother of the famous poetess and hymn writer Fanny Crosby. Although this woman's husband died before Fanny was even 12 months old, she lived past 91.

Fanny was born perfectly healthy in every way. When she was six weeks old, she caught a slight cold that caused an inflammation in her eyes. The family physician was out of town, so Fanny's mother called another doctor to attend to her. He recommended a remedy that destroyed little Fanny's eyesight.

This is what Fanny wrote of him in her autobiography:

> But I have not for a moment, in more than eighty-five years, felt a spark of resentment against him, because I have always believed from my youth to this very moment that the good Lord, in his infinite mercy, by this means, consecrated me to the work that I am still permitted to do. When I remember his mercy and lovingkindness; when I have been blessed above the common lot of mortals; and when happiness has touched the deep places of my soul, how can I repine?[6]

There is no doubt that Fanny's Presbyterian mother and grandmother influenced her mind-set in this regard. Fanny had a love for life and for Christ. Her attitude is reflected in this personal statement: "It has always been my favorite theory that the blind can accomplish nearly everything that may be done by those who can see. Do not think that those who are deprived of physical vision are shut out from the best that earth has to offer her children."[7]

Fanny grew up in the country, about which she says, "To a young and imaginative person there is nothing more inspiring than life in the country. Existence becomes a perpetual dream of delight; and there are no pangs to sadden the buoyant spirit."[8] However, with all that the country and the local village school had to offer her, she longed to know more. She often prayed for the Lord to show her how she could learn like other children.

The answer to the prayer of her heart, and the release from her mother, arrived on the same day when she was almost 15 years old. She says that as her mother read the letter of acceptance from the New York Institution for the Blind, she clapped her hands and exclaimed, "Oh, thank God, He has answered my prayer, just as I knew He would." Fanny continues in her autobiography, "This was the happiest day of my life; for the dark intellectual maze in which I had been living seemed to yield to hope and the promise of the light that was about to dawn…The New York Institution was a foreign name to me, but it was enough to know that some place existed where I might be taught; and my star of promise even then was becoming a great orb of light." [9]

In her personal story she adds,

> My mother was fully conscious of my joy, but to test me she said, "What will you do without me? You have never been away from home for more than two weeks at one time in your whole life." This presented a new idea: I had not thought of the separation from her; and for a moment I wavered. Then I answered as bravely as I could, "Much as I love you, Mother, I am willing to make any sacrifice to acquire an education." And she replied, "You are right, my child, and I am very glad you have the chance to go." But her voice betrayed the tremor in her heart. How wonderful is a mother's love. [10]

I'm sure this mother's release was a challenging one, for she had no husband to console her, and she had been the sole caretaker of Fanny for nearly 15 years. Although she would remain at home alone, she had rewarding years ahead. Truly, love brings about a fruit-bearing release.

Although Fanny had written poetry from the time she was a child, she didn't write her first hymn until she was 44 years old. From that time on, until she died, she wrote almost 9,000 hymns, often three within a week's time. Among them are such well-known hymns as "Blessed Assurance," "All the Way My Savior Leads Me" and "Rescue the Perishing."

Fanny could quote the entire Pentateuch, all four Gospels, Proverbs, Ruth, Song of Solomon and part of the book of Psalms. She often said that her goal was to lead one million people to Christ before she died. She died at the age of 95. One has to wonder if, through her hymns, she accomplished her goal.

A mother's release of her teen is emotionally challenging and sacrificial. It requires trust in the Lord and in that which she has already imparted to the child. Is it significant and potentially fruitful? Most definitely.

A mother's release of her teen is emotionally challenging and sacrificial. It requires trust in the Lord and in that which she has already imparted to the child.

There is another mother I know who released her teen in a different way. Night after night she watched her teen come home with a troubled countenance. She would ask him a few questions about his day but received little response. She was, as many mothers are in this season, reduced to prayer. There are no more attentive ears than the ones that listen to a mother's prayers.

This mother could not easily discern her son's personal quandary. He was a star athlete and at the top of his class academically, and he played an instrument in a lead position in the school band. Not only did he have all of these accomplishments going for him, he was also respected by his teachers and friends who were true buddies and girls who were easily flattered by his attention.

Even though the Lord had favored him with all of these wonderful blessings, she noticed that he rarely seemed happy, especially at church. He had received Christ as his personal Savior when he was a young child. As a teen, he was obedient and honored his parents by attending services, but his heart wasn't in it. When she tried to draw him out, her son was polite but withdrawn from any family conversation that had any genuine depth.

One night, when they had out-of-town overnight guests in their home, he came in around ten o'clock in the evening and then left again within a few minutes "to go for a walk." She had noticed his troubled countenance as he came and left, but she attempted to remain focused on her guests. After they went to bed, she went to prayer. As she prayed, she sensed the Lord's assurance that her son was in His hands and that he would return, not only physically but spiritually as well. She went to bed trusting, not in her son, but in her Lord.

She didn't know how deeply entrenched her son was in a double-standard lifestyle, appearing one way to his parents and another to his friends at school. She didn't know how this pattern was replacing his faith with confusion and pain. She didn't know that if she had pressed him on the concerns of his heart he would have left. She had no awareness of the self-destructive behavior he was engaged in. She didn't know that he was seriously contemplating suicide that dark and lonely night, and if she had pressed him, his despair would have swallowed up his life. But she did know the God she had dedicated her son to many years prior. Yes, her confidence rested in God, not in her son. The main key to successfully releasing your teen is to release the teen and embrace the Master.

> *The main key to successfully releasing your teen is to release the teen and embrace the Master.*

Within a few days, a beloved aunt and uncle came to visit. The aunt, who was endeared to the teen, and a praying woman herself, had a very insightful conversation with her nephew. The Lord had revealed to her in prayer the young man's struggles. She, in turn, revealed to him her knowledge of the battles going on in his heart and the Lord's answers to those struggles. Not long after their conversation, this teenager made a distinct turnaround and made clear choices to follow the Lord. Today he is a fruitful minister of the Gospel and mentor to many teens and young adults.

Did this young man's mother need to release her teen even when she wanted to hold him more tightly? Yes. Did she need to release him to seek and find God for himself in this tenuous season of his life? Yes. Was it hard? Did it create anxious moments within her own spirit? Was it scary? Yes to all of the above. Was there any other way? Probably not. Eventually, he would need to find God for himself.

Did this son already know his mother's perspective on the issues he was struggling with? Yes. This was part of his greatest struggle. Would he, at this point, have listened to her repeat to him the values she held most dear? Yes, but he wouldn't have adhered to them. Did he want to hurt and disappoint her? Most assuredly not. Did he desperately need and even want her prayers? Most definitely, even when he struggled against them just as an unbroken stallion does when he resists the master's bridling. Would he have made it without her faithful prayers? That is questionable, at best.

If you have a teen in your home or in your life, regardless of where they are in their personal commitment to Christ, if you have never released them into the care of the heavenly Father, take a moment now and offer them up to God in prayer. After you've done this, begin to treasure this trust and watch God work in their lives.

If you have offered your child to the Lord numerous times and he or she is still struggling desperately, renew your trust and embrace the Master afresh. The Lord wants you to know that "You, dear children, are from God and have overcome them, because the One who is in you is greater than the one who is in the world" (1 John 4:4).

Like Mary, if you have spoken out of frustration and anxiousness to your teen, but he or she has not been able to put it into proper perspective, ask for their forgiveness. Whether forgiveness is given in return or not, continue on in your love, for the Scripture reads for you today, "This then is how we know that we belong to the truth, and how we set our hearts at rest in his presence whenever our hearts condemn us. For God is greater than our hearts, and he knows everything" (1 John 3:19,20).

Were the hearts of the mother of this confused and rebellious teen and Fanny Crosby's mother woven together with Mary's in Jerusalem that day so many years ago? In some huge way I think they were.

Luke 2:51,52 says that following this event when Jesus was 12, "Then he went down to Nazareth with them and was obedient to them. But his mother treasured all these things in her heart. And Jesus grew in wisdom and stature, and in favor with God and men." He went home and submitted to His parents and their input for 18 years.

Yes, this was the day Jesus discovered who He was. However, it was also the day he chose to demonstrate to mankind throughout the ages the importance of honoring your parents and not despising daily life, for both are seedbeds of preparation for the future.

We need to ponder this moment of release as a hidden treasure in our hearts and let our teens' knowledge of who their father is go beyond that of their earthly father to their heavenly Father. Release, trust, treasure, for therein lies your teen's solid foundation and hope in Christ for the next season of life. And therein lies the hidden power of a mother's heart.

Pondering the Pathways

LUKE 2:19: *"But Mary kept all these things and pondered them in her heart." (NKJV)*

PROVERBS 4:25,26: *"Let your eyes look straight ahead, and your eyelids look right before you. Ponder the path of your feet, and let all your ways be established." (NKJV)*

PROVERBS 5:1-6: *"My son, pay attention to my wisdom; lend your ear to my understanding, that you may preserve discretion, and your lips may keep knowledge. For the lips of an immoral woman drip honey, and her mouth is smoother than oil; but in the end she is bitter as wormwood, sharp as a two-edged sword. Her feet go down to death, her steps lay hold of hell. Lest you ponder her path of life—her ways are unstable; you do not know them." (NKJV)*

PROVERBS 5:21: *"For the ways of man are before the eyes of the Lord, and He ponders all his paths." (NKJV)*

PSALMS 17:5: *"My steps have held fast to Your paths, my feet have not slipped." (NASB)*

PSALMS 23:3: *"He guides me in the paths of righteousness for His name's sake." (NASB)*

PSALMS 25:4: *"Make me know Your ways, O Lord; teach me Your paths."*

PSALMS 25:10: *"All the paths of the Lord are lovingkindness and truth to those who keep His covenant and His testimonies." (NASB)*

PROVERBS 2:7,8: *"He stores up sound wisdom for the upright; He is a shield to those who walk in integrity, guarding the paths of justice, and He preserves the way of His godly ones." (NASB)*

PROVERBS 2:20-22: *"So you will walk in the way of good men and keep to the paths of the righteous. For the upright will live in the land and the blameless will remain in it; but the wicked will be cut off from the land and the treacherous will be uprooted from it." (NASB)*

PROVERBS 3:6: *"In all your ways acknowledge Him, and He will make your paths straight." (NASB)*

PROVERBS 3:13,17: *"How blessed is the man who finds wisdom and the man who gains understanding...her ways are pleasant ways and all her paths are peace." (NASB)*

NOTES

1   *"Altogether, Jerusalem covered, at its greatest, about 300 acres. ....Ancient Jewish writings enable us to identify no fewer than 118 different articles of import from foreign lands, covering more than even modern luxury has devised. ...Its population, computed at from 200,000 to 250,000, was enormously swelled by travellers, and by pilgrims during the great festivals. The great Palace was the residence of King and Court, with all their following and luxury; in Antonia lay afterwards the Roman garrison. The Temple called thousands of priests, any of them with their families, to Jerusalem; while learned Academies were filled with hundreds, though it may have been mostly poor, scholars and students. In Jerusalem must have been many of the large warehouses for the near commercial harbour of Joppa; and thence, as from the industrial centres of busy Galilee, would the pedlar go forth to carry his wares over the land. More especially would the markets of Jerusalem, held, however, in bazaars and streets rather than in squares, be thronged with noisy sellers and bargaining buyers."* Alfred Edersheim, *The Life and Times of Jesus the Messiah*, (Peabody, Massachusetts 01961, Hendrickson Publishers, 1993), p. 81,82.

2   Luke 2:48, *The Message Bible*

3   Luke 2:49, *The Message Bible*

4   *"In going to these great feasts, families and neighbours would join together, and form a large collection."* Albert Barnes, *Barnes' Notes on the New Testament*, (Grand Rapids, Michigan 49503, Kregel Publications, 1962, 1963, 1966), p. 192.

5   Isa. 1:18, NIV

6   Fanny J. Crosby, *Fanny J. Crosby: An Autobiography*, (Grand Rapids, Mich.: Baker Book House, 1986), p. 24.

7   Ibid., p. 22.

8   Ibid., p. 35.

9   Ibid., p. 44.

10 Ibid., p. 46.

Releasing into Adulthood

On the third day a wedding took place at Cana in Galilee. Jesus' mother was there, and Jesus and his disciples had also been invited to the wedding. When the wine was gone, Jesus' mother said to him, "They have no more wine." "Dear woman, why do you involve me?" Jesus replied. "My time has not yet come." His mother said to the servants, "Do whatever he tells you." Nearby stood six stone water jars, the kind used by the Jews for ceremonial washing, each holding from twenty to thirty gallons. Jesus said to the servants, "Fill the jars with water;" so they filled them to the brim. Then he told them, "Now draw some out and take it to the master of the banquet." They did so, and the master of the banquet tasted the water that had been turned into wine. He did not realize where it had come from, though the servants who had drawn the water knew. Then he called the bridegroom aside and said, "Everyone brings out the choice wine first and then the cheaper wine after the guests have had too much to drink; but you have saved the best till now." This, the first of his miraculous signs, Jesus performed at Cana in Galilee. He thus revealed his glory, and his disciples put their faith in him. — John 2:1-11

Weary from the late night festivities of the previous six evenings, Mary had slipped back to her room intending to rest for a few minutes. She wanted to be sure she had enough energy to keep up with all of the excitement throughout the last grand evening of the wedding celebration. She looked radiant in her royal blue head covering with wisps of graying curls framing her face.

As she approached the women's quarters which were located just off the kitchen area and near where the wine was stored, she overheard the servants whispering to each other about the shortage of wine. To run out of wine at a wedding would be a social *faux pas* that would long be remembered in the small town of Cana. It was, in fact, the kind of social blunder that could become the subject of mockery and ridicule, not only in the local neighborhood, but also in the neighboring towns for years to come.

When the servants and banquet master realized that she had overheard their conversation, they were panic-stricken. But she assured them that she would pray for a miracle. Assured that she was harmless, they turned back away from her and resumed their harried conversation about what to do.

Mary felt terrible for her friends as well as the banquet master. She did not want either of them to bear this great humiliation. The master of the banquet would be held ultimately responsible for such a fatal error, however it would reflect directly on the family. Immediately she turned into her quarters to pray, but couldn't as there was another woman resting quietly on another cot in the same room. She left and went out to the veranda and began to pray. *Oh, dear Father, my poor friend and her husband are out of wine! You know what that means; they are in dire need!*

She continued her plea, *I have never complained about our lifestyle and the way we have had to pinch pennies, but I sure would like to be able to help my friends, Lord. You know what the gossips will do with this. My friends will never live it down and the master of the banquet will likely lose his job and his reputation!*

Guests usually helped to defray the costs of the seven-day wedding feast with their gifts and their money. She, being poor, had not been able to help financially, so this was her opportunity to help. Although she felt terrible for her friends, she felt thankful that she had overheard the need.

Even though Mary was older now, closer to 50 than to 40 as a matter of fact, she was still a woman who was energized by helping to meet a need. When she saw a need, she desired to help meet that need in any way that she could. She also still had a personality that sparkled with verve and determination. She was, in fact, willing to barge in where others might fear to tread.

She prayerfully paced the veranda one more time, and then went back inside the house and resumed her prayerful march in the hallway between the main receiving room and the kitchen. As she continued to pace back and forth near the doorway and the kitchen, she prayed silently. Suddenly, she saw Jesus and his new disciples coming down the pathway to the house. They too had taken a brief respite from the crowd and gone down by the lakeside to rest and fellowship alone for a short while in the late afternoon. Her heart leaped!

She knew that Jesus would know what to do. He had been such an amazing provider for her and the younger children since Joseph's death; surely He would know what to do now. She walked toward them through the now early-evening crowd.

Knowing that she had gone to rest, when Jesus saw her coming toward him, he was instantly attuned to the fact that she looked distressed, not rested. Rather than carrying herself with her usual grace and dignity, she darted in and out of socializing guests rather frantically. *What could it be,* he wondered? *Could something have happened to one of his younger siblings?*

"Jesus, son, they're just about out of wine! You know what that could mean!" Mary said frenetically. *"Mom, how is that our business—yours or mine? This isn't my time; please, don't be pushy."* Jesus said in response. Distracted by the immediate need at hand, it was as if she didn't hear a word he said. She simply turned to the two closest servants nearby, made

a gesture toward Jesus and said, *"Do whatever he tells you to do."* She walked on down the hall towards the main receiving room, assured that the mission was accomplished. While she walked away she pondered, not what he said, but how he said it. *That tone of voice, what was that? I haven't heard that tone for years. ..... In fact, it was 18 years ago at Passover, when Joseph and I found him on the Temple steps, that I last heard that tone in his voice. What could it mean?* It was as if she could see old Simeon's sword in her mind's eye with the word *'RELEASE'* engraved on it. Humbly, she whispered, *"Yes, Father; yes, I release him to do Your bidding, not mine."*

Out of the corner of her eye, she could see Jesus telling the servants to do something. They immediately went and filled six stoneware water pots, twenty to thirty gallons each with water and brought them to him. As they returned the pots in front of him, she caught his eye; with a look of adoration and release she smiled, as did he in return. He then turned, prayed, and instructed the servants to take the vessels to the master of the banquet for his approval.

Have you ever asked your adult children to do something for someone, but they weren't motivated to do it? Have you ever neglected to realize that your adult children may have their own ideas about how a situation should be handled, and you were surprised when they let you know it?

If you've ever had a responsible single adult child live with you for very long, you probably can identify with these questions and with Mary at the wedding in Cana. You often still have a certain amount of input in your young adult's life, especially when he or she is still living with you. At the same time, as you get accustomed to them carrying part of the adult household responsibilities, it's easy to become dependent on them in certain areas.

How long should adult children continue to do what you say, and when should you release them to do as they think they should? In other words, when do you shift from specifically directing them and transition into advising them? Your role as a parent and theirs as an adult child can be confusing at times to say the least.

Cana was approximately six miles northeast of Nazareth. Mary obviously was well acquainted with the host and hostess of the wedding. Some scholars believe she may have even been related to this family. Hence, she would not have wanted them to suffer the horrible embarrassment of running out of wine.

The wedding host was responsible for providing his guests with adequate wine for seven days, but he would relegate the banquet details to a designated master of the banquet. This person was considered to be in a position of honor, and one of his primary duties was to regulate the distribution of wine. He would also monitor the wine and the guests for any incident that might ruin the party.

Usually the purest wine was served first and then the wine that had been diluted with water would be served later in the week when palates were less discerning and brain cells were in need of moderation. To run out of wine was considered to be such a social failure that it ran the risk of damaging the family's reputation. To have this happen in a small town such as Cana, with closely-knit neighboring towns, could have been devastating to the family name for years. This would be a disaster for the hosts as well as for the new bride and groom.

It is probable that Mary had been a widow for a number of years by this time. Most likely, this meant one of two things, or perhaps even both. Firstly, she was used to being aware of the needs of a household and making sure that those needs were met. That meant, she was also used to being in charge of a household. Secondly, she was used to Jesus, as the firstborn son, helping to meet those needs. He must have been a very attentive and responsible son, as she obviously had complete confidence that He would know what to do about the situation at hand.

It doesn't appear that Mary took his response as an insult or an unwillingness to meet the need, or she would not have instructed the servants to do whatever he told them to do. Even though this is an obvious moment of release between Mary and Jesus, it was not meant to be harsh. In fact, the term "woman" is the same term in which he tenderly addressed her later while on the Cross. If this was a reproof to Mary, it was a mild one and didn't wound her or hinder her from continuing to believe that He would still provide an answer for her concern. If anything, this was a mild reproof for Mary's attempt to direct his steps when it was time for him to be hearing direction from his heavenly Father directly.

It's interesting to note that it was when this mother saw a need that the embarking of her son's ministry took place and the first miracle was released. Mary's perception of a need kicked into gear at exactly the same time that Jesus' first major adult ministry transaction was to take place.

I think our heavenly Father has equipped mothers with the ability to be aware of numerous needs that surround them and their children. He does this for a variety of reasons I'm sure. One reason is perhaps, just as this one was for Mary and Jesus, to enable the necessary release into the next season of life and ministry.

Even though Mary must have felt that Jesus' words had cut the emotional umbilical cord, so to speak, it's amazing how persistent and full of faith she remained. Some might say 'stubborn,' but I prefer to think her seeming oversight of Jesus' statement and her continuing comment to the servants was a statement of faith. She was acting in confidence that Jesus had heard her concern and would provide what was necessary.

You could easily liken her to other Old Testament pursuers of God who didn't take no for an answer. Consider Jacob in Genesis 32:22-32 when he wrestled with the messenger of God and wouldn't let him go until he received a blessing. Moses persisted with God on behalf of the people until God made a covenant with him in Exodus 33:12-34:10. Elijah was also an example for Mary in 1 Kings 18:36-38 when he cried out, "Answer me, O Lord, answer me," and then fire fell from heaven and burned up Elijah's sacrifice. And what about Elisha in 2 Kings 4:8-37, when he beseeched God to raise the Shunammite widow's son from the dead?

Had not Mary followed her ancestors' example in asking in faith, believing that it would happen? Yes, she was demonstrating that same strong faith and tenacity manifested throughout the generations of her people.

She had spoken faith, but then came the time to release faith that the petition she had made had been heard and would be answered. When Jesus spoke the word, she had to release him to be the adult he was. In doing so, it required of her to release her son into his next season of life, one step further away and yet one step closer. As we release our children from their childhood, we invite them into adult friendship with us. Jesus would transition from being her natural provider to becoming her spiritual provider.

As we release our children from their childhood,
we invite them into adult friendship with us.

As the dean of women at a Bible college, I've watched a lot of mothers over the years go through the releasing-into-adulthood phase. Some wait anxiously and nervously in registration lines all day. Some busy themselves by carrying boxes from home, wanting desperately to arrange their son's or daughter's dorm room, only to realize the "child" wants to do it his or her way. Some sit on the lawn just outside the men's dorms and long to march right into the rooms of their sons, whom they know are hopelessly lost when it comes to arranging a room, only to be told, "Wait outside, Mom; you're embarrassing me." Some mothers are excited with the prospect that college life will help their child grow up. The countenances of others reveal that the nest is empty all too soon.

Two things are sure to happen when it comes to this type of release: First, when you least expect it, your emotions will show up. Second, your emotional down times will come at different times than when your best friend's do. Seldom compare emotional responses with another mother's and don't try to advise your friend about how to release her child into adulthood. Her response may be completely different from yours and vice versa.

Most mothers go through a range of emotions as they release their children into adulthood. Some mothers who enroll their young adult children into university drive away in tears; some drive away in relief. Some mothers rejoice about university but struggle with the release into marriage. Some mothers rejoice when their children take to the marriage aisle but struggle with the adventures that their adult children want to take when they are single.

Most mothers go through a range of emotions
as they release their children into adulthood.

I had such a release myself one summer. My young adult daughter, Angie, responded to an opportunity to spend her summer doing a ministerial internship under a seasoned missionary in Cambodia. She was excited with zeal for the Lord and with the spirit of adventure burning in her heart. She and another classmate made the long journey together. Angie would stay for the summer; her classmate Jenny would stay for a year.

A feeling of release was at the forefront of my heart and my trust level was high. I had always encouraged her to do something with her singleness, not just something about it. In other words, I encouraged her to enjoy her single years and do something effective and fulfilling for the Lord before she got married. That all sounds good when you're saying it, but it's different when you're living it. However, I really meant it. She was going to be with people that we knew to be very wise and competent and I felt good about it.

Angie's assignments while there varied from taking language classes to teaching piano lessons, Bible studies and various other things.

Although Cambodian mosquitoes seemed to be attracted to her American body, she easily adapted to the culture and the heat and humidity of the area. She also quickly developed good friendships with some other young women who were there serving from the Philippines.

One late afternoon, after being there for just a couple of weeks, the girls decided to go into town to have a nice dinner. The mode of hired transportation in Phnom Penh is moto-taxies, taxies that are small motorcycles. The missionary had warned Angie and Jenny to never stay out past dark because they were white Caucasians, an easy target for thieves. The Filipinos would not be as easily noticed because of their Asian faces and skin tone.

The dinner in town and fellowship with the other girls was wonderful. The time had been filled with laughter, good food and sweet fellowship. By the time they left the restaurant, it was dark outside. They all hailed taxies and each went their own direction. Angie was on a moto-taxi with one of the Filipino girls, and Jenny was on another.

On a side street, six thieves stopped the taxi Angie was on. Although she could not understand what they were saying, anytime she tried to say something aloud in English or Khmer, they would tap her on the forehead and look at her in a threatening manner. When she prayed or spoke the name of Jesus aloud, it was as if they didn't even hear her supplications to the Lord. They tried to get the new camera she had attached on a shoulder strap, and when she resisted, they put a gun in her ribs. In rather delayed wisdom, she released the camera. They took all of the jewelry off of the other girl except her earrings. She quickly removed those before they ripped them out of her ears.

In that moment of terror, Angie had a small sign of the Lord's ever-watchful eye. When she was 13 years old, her father had given her a special ring. It signified a covenant made between the two of them with a challenge for her to maintain her moral purity and to give her heart to no other man until he had given his blessing for her to do so. The ring represented a very special connection of love and purity between them. Even though the thieves insisted on stealing all of the other girl's jewelry, it was as though they were blinded to the special covenant ring on Angie's finger. To her, this was evidence that the Lord was indeed watching over her.

The next day was Father's Day in America. Angie phoned home early that morning and began the conversation with "Happy Father's Day, Dad. I have something to tell you…." As we both sat and listened to her story, it seemed as though a hundred emotions ran through my heart and mind colliding with each other. I heard her say the words that she was okay, but I just wanted her back in my arms where I could embrace her and make her feel safe again, like a child tucked into bed at night. I wanted to be calm and offer her courage, and yet I wanted to weep woman-to-woman as I empathetically felt the violation of her personal safety.

What should I offer this now young adult daughter; the courage to stay or an airline ticket to return home? Should I tell her to be brave or to retreat? Should I chide her for not obeying the missionary more specifically or offer her comfort and understanding? Should I treat her like a teen that should return home under my tutelage or like an adult who should remain released to hear from God herself?

Should I treat her like a teen that should return home under my tutelage or like an adult who should remain released to hear from God herself?

A couple of weeks after this event, internal national turmoil began to heat up within the capital city of Phnom Penh. The two prime ministers had been enemies for years. One finally found an opportunity to stage a coup while the other one was out of the country. The military generals of the army of the prime minister who was out of the country at the time lived just down the street from where the missionaries and girls were living. There was war in the streets. It was the first time in Angie's life that she ever heard "real cannon fire on the Fourth of July," much to her delight.

Other nations were extracting their people from the nation of Cambodia. Even her Filipino comrades had to depart at their homeland's request. Although some Americans in other parts of the nation were leaving, America had not yet officially demanded that American citizens leave the nation.

We kept in touch through e-mails and phone calls. Again, what should we as parents do? Should we demand that she return to our definition of safety, or should we allow her to hear our counsel and then make her own decision? Again, my emotions found their moments of calmness and questioning, as well as fear and faith. We prayed; she prayed; we released; she stayed. She finished her exciting adventure and truly embarked on the realities of the adult world.

Was she dedicated to the Lord as a baby? Yes. Was she released as an adult? Yes, that too. Is this journey of a mother's heart an easy process? Yes and no; trusting in the heavenly Father and His canopy of protection is the safest place any child could ever be – even an adult child. It is in that hidden place, your personal place of prayer, that you have influence in your adult children's lives. Is it easy to do? Perhaps not. Is it full of abiding peace and joy? Most definitely.

It is in that hidden place, your personal place of prayer, that you have influence in your adult children's lives.

My heart that summer was once again intertwined with Mary's as I said to my daughter, *'Do whatever He tells you to do.'* It wasn't comfortable and it wasn't easy; but it was the wisdom of God and the safest place for her to be.

There is coming a day, if it has not already come, when you must release your child into adulthood. You must not hold on any longer, for your son or daughter is not a child to be molded by your daily care, but rather an adult to be influenced by your daily release. Do it today and watch the miracle unfold before your very eyes. There really is hidden power in a mother's heart.

The Safety of the Lord

LEVITICUS 25:18: *"So you shall observe My statutes and keep My judgments, and perform them; and you will dwell in the land in safety." (NKJV)*

DEUTERONOMY 33:12: *"The beloved of the Lord shall dwell in safety by Him, Who shelters him all the day long; and he shall dwell between His shoulders." (NKJV)*

PSALMS 4:8: *"I will both lie down in peace, and sleep; for You alone, O Lord, make me dwell in safety." (NKJV)*

PROVERBS 11:14: *"Where there is no counsel, the people fall; but in the multitude of counselors there is safety." (NKJV)*

GENESIS 31:49: *"May the Lord watch between you and me when we are absent one from another." (NKJV)*

PSALMS 12:7: *"You shall keep them, O Lord, You shall preserve them from this generation forever." (NKJV)*

PSALMS 91:11: *"For He shall give His angels charge over you, to keep you in all your ways." (NKJV)*

PROVERBS 3:1,2: *"My son, do not forget my law, but let your heart keep my commands; for length of days and long life and peace they will add to you." (NKJV)*

Releasing into Destiny

Near the cross of Jesus stood his mother, his mother's sister, Mary the wife of Clopas, and Mary Magdalene. When Jesus saw his mother there, and the disciple whom he loved standing nearby, he said to his mother, "Dear woman, here is your son," and to the disciple, "Here is your mother." From that time on, this disciple took her into his home. — John 19:25-27

They all joined together constantly in prayer, along with the women and Mary the mother of Jesus, and with his brothers. — Acts 1:14

The scream inside her head was silenced by the sheer terror of what she could see from a distance. Tears streamed from her eyes like a waterfall as sobs came from a place so deep within her that they could not be heard. She could have never imagined such agony. The nightmare of watching her firstborn son being stripped and beaten beyond recognition sent a sword so deeply into her soul that she could not stand. She lay on the street in the middle of the throng of hate-filled people with only a handful of friends by her side.

This release was beyond anything that God had asked of her before. She felt from deep within that she would never recover; the agony was deeper than the darkest night and shredded every fiber of her being.

Mary knew that among certain elements of the population, hostility had been growing toward her firstborn son. But there were so many that loved him, so many who had been miraculously touched by him that she never dreamed it would come to this. How could those who loved him so ever allow something so hideous, so torturous to come to her beloved son?

She had refused to listen to the negative reports that had been heard coming out of Jerusalem. However admittedly, in recent days, her heart had been continuously guided back to the prophet Isaiah. His words seemed to have been her constant meditation of late.

He was despised and rejected by men, a man of sorrows, and familiar with suffering. Like one from whom men hide their faces he was despised, and we esteemed him not. Surely he took up our infirmities and carried our sorrows, yet we considered him stricken by God, smitten by him, and afflicted. But he was pierced for our transgressions, he was crushed for our iniquities; the punishment that brought us peace was upon him and by his wounds we are healed. We all like sheep, have gone astray, each of us has turned to his own way; and the Lord has laid on him the iniquity of us all. He was oppressed and afflicted, yet he did not open his mouth; he was led like a lamb to the slaughter, and as a sheep before her shearers is silent, so he did not open his mouth.[1]

There were no angels to prepare her heart this time. Only the voice of her firstborn son could penetrate the deep sorrow she felt. Should she go to Calvary? *Could* she go to Calvary? She must. But how could she bear to look upon his tortured body for even one more moment? Her mind was full, but the pain of the reality she faced numbed her thoughts.

As the soldiers began to lead Jesus from the whipping post to the roadway to Calvary, Mary could feel two of her friends lift her by the arms up to her feet. They linked arms and began to slowly make their way through the crowd so they could keep their eyes on Jesus. Mary began to cry out from within, *Oh Father, bless and strengthen my son, Your Son, for this burden that he must bear.*

Though my mind is numb, my heart is exploding. My legs move like weighted iron. I reach for one thought and it evaporates before I can grasp it. I reach for another to bring me reason and it eludes me as well. Feeling emotionally paralyzed, she quit thinking and just kept putting one foot in front of the other as the others helped her along. Although she wasn't fifty years old yet, she felt and walked as though she were twice her age. The weight of the emotional pain that she bore was more than she could endure.

As she trudged up the streets to Calvary's hill with her eyes locked onto her beloved son, her mind flashed back to the first moment she ever held him in her arms. She could almost feel the ecru and purple swaddling cloths as her fingers thoughtlessly stroked her headcovering. He was so precious, so perfect to behold. Next, she could see him toddling to her and gleefully falling into her waiting arms. If only she could reach him now. If only she could take his place.

The crowd was unbearable, taunting and cruel. She closed her eyes and put her hands over her ears to prevent their words from penetrating her heart. In an instant, she could see him at twelve, sitting on the Temple steps, amazing the priests with his words and his questions. She could see his penetrating eyes looking into hers, longing for her to understand when he said that he had to "be about his Father's business." Oh, how she longed to put her arms around him again and turn him away from Jerusalem back toward Nazareth and the simple life of a carpenter's shop.

Startled back into reality, she looked and realized that he had stumbled under the weight of the cross and the soldiers commanded a man in the crowd to carry the heavy beam for him. Their eyes met again, just before the soldier cracked his whip at him to move on. As his eyes met hers, she could once again see his first miracle at the wedding in Cana—such a gesture of kindness and compassion. As the soldier's whip lashed against his already open flesh once again, she was bolted back into reality. She could hardly bear it another moment; her sweet memories of her beloved son were being splattered with pain with each crack of the whip.

After what seemed to be an eternity of agonizing torture watching Jesus struggle to reach Calvary's hill, the soldiers threw him to the ground and she collapsed as if they had done the same to her. As she watched them nail him to the Cross and stand it up for all to see his shame, deep groaning as had never before been heard came from the depths of her soul. She bowed herself to the ground and sobbed uncontrollably, throwing dirt up in the air; she cared little who heard her or what they thought of her. Her soul was in deep grief and agony. She longed to cover his shame and minister healing to his wounds, but knew that there was nothing she could do to bring him comfort from this cruel Cross.

From deep within, she cried out, *can I bear this, my soul?* "*My tears have been my food day and night, while men say to me all day long, 'Where is your God?' These things I remember as I pour out my soul: how I used to go with the multitude, leading the procession to the house of God, with shouts of joy and thanksgiving among the festive throng. Why are you downcast, O my soul? Why so disturbed within me? Put your hope in God, for I will yet praise him, my Savior and my God.*" [2]

As the words of the psalmist erupted from her soul, the realization of who her beloved son truly was overwhelmed her. She slowly stood, at the sound of his voice, and heard him say to his young disciple John that he should consider her as his mother. Then he looked into her eyes and tenderly told her to consider John as her son.

The final release had come, the final thrust of Simeon's sword penetrated her whole being with pain. And yet, the realization that he was now her Savior miraculously eclipsed the reality that he was her son. A mysterious peace entered her heart through grief's door. She knew in that moment that she would see him again soon, not as he was, but as he had been and would forever be, for truly he was the Son of God.

As she, John and the others walked away from the Cross, after Joseph of Arimathea came and recovered his body, she could hear the whisper of the Father. *"Well done, highly favored one."* *"Father,"* she whispered, *"Highly favored? … Yes,…yes, I am highly favored ."*

The realization that he was now her Savior miraculously eclipsed the reality that he was her son.

I doubt that we can really begin to comprehend what must have gone through Mary's heart and spirit that day. But neither can any one individual grasp the emotional pain another goes through at a time of release like this.

It's abhorrent to any mother to consider the possibility of her child's death before her own. When it does happen, how does one cope?

At the loss of a beloved 11 month old daughter, Pastor Jack Louman, had someone say to him with deep compassion, *"Life is not a puzzle to be solved, it's a mystery to be lived by faith."* How true this is. We cannot, with our own minds, always figure life out as it is presented to us; we simply must leave the mystery of it in God's hands and live it by faith.

"Life is not a puzzle to be solved, it's a mystery to be lived by faith."

"We live our lives in a world marked by assumptions. We wake up in the morning and *assume* that life will be much as it was yesterday. We go to bed and wake up expecting the sun to rise. Our children go off to school and come home again at the end of the school day. We go to work and return at the end of our work day expecting our home and our possessions to be there when we return. We *assume* our good health, daily interactions with loved ones, co-workers and friends, and the business-as-usual routine in our job and community. When illness, tragedy, or catastrophic events happen to us or to someone we care about, our world of assumption is threatened, if not shattered." [3]

Assumptions will shatter you, but faith will get you through life's twists and turns. Assumptions will rob you of the influence you have as a mother. They will steal from you the joy of releasing your child into his or her ultimate destiny, because to do so means change. Assumptions fruitlessly cling to today refusing to recognize tomorrow. Assumptions lie. They tell you that things will always be the same. That is a lie. Life is progressive, not static. Life demands that you progress, the choice of how you do that is up to you.

Life is progressive, not static. Life demands that you progress, the choice of how you do that is up to you.

I recently heard a news broadcast in which a married couple and their seven-year-old son were vacationing in Europe. One evening, as they were driving, some gunmen accosted them, shot at their car and attempted to force them off the road. In the harrowing process, their seven-year-old son, Nicholas, was shot while sleeping in the backseat.

After arriving at the hospital and learning that Nicholas would not survive, a doctor approached them, with a request for them to consider donating his organs. They prayerfully decided this was the best decision given the circumstances, as grievous and painful as they were. The seven-year-olds' kidneys were soon transplanted into the body of a young single woman who was hoping to soon be married. A year after Nicholas' death, the now young married woman gave birth to a baby boy and named him Nicholas, after her life-saving benefactor.

Nicholas' mother released her son in death and chose blessing for his legacy. She chose to allow life to come out of that excruciatingly painful release. Her son lives on today through the life of this healthy young mother and her son.

In 1873, another husband and wife were traveling with their children. The husband was a Christian lawyer from Chicago, Illinois, named Horatio Spafford. He traveled with his wife and four young children to the city of New York, where he had some business to attend before embarking upon further travel. Upon arriving in New York, Mr. Spafford took his wife and children to the boarding docks to put them onto the luxury liner *Ville de Havre* that was sailing to France. He planned to join them in about three or four weeks, after he finished some business in New York City.

The voyage started out beautifully. But on the evening of November 21, 1873, as the *Ville de Havre* proceeded peacefully across the Atlantic Ocean, the ship was struck by another vessel, the *Lochearn*. Thirty minutes later it sank to the ocean floor with the loss of nearly all on board.

When the announcement came that the ship was sinking, Mrs. Spafford knelt with her children and prayed that they might either be saved or be willing to die if that was God's will. A few minutes later, in the terror and confusion, three of the children were swept away by the ocean waves while she stood clutching the youngest child, a baby girl. Suddenly the baby was swept from her arms. As she reached for her, she caught the baby by her gown; but then another wave came quickly and swept her away forever. Mrs. Spafford fell unconscious and awakened later to find that she had been rescued by sailors from the *Lochearn*, but the four children were gone.

It was 10 days before the *Lochearn* arrived in Cardiff where Mrs. Spafford could send a message to her husband in New York City. He had heard of the sinking of the *Ville de Havre* and was waiting anxiously to receive word. The word came: "Saved alone." That night he paced the floor in anguish and prayed to the Lord he knew and trusted. Miraculously, he found that peace that surpasses all understanding. [4]

Sometime later, after being reunited with his wife, he wrote the well-known hymn "It Is Well with My Soul."

When peace, like a river, attendeth my way,
When sorrows like sea billows roll;
Whatever my lot, thou hast taught me to say,
It is well, it is well with my soul.

Though Satan should buffet, though trials should come;
Let this blest assurance control;
That Christ has regarded my helpless estate,
And has shed his own blood for my soul.

My sin—O the bliss of this glorious thought!
My sin, not in part, but the whole,
Is nailed to the cross and I bear it no more;
Praise the Lord, praise the Lord, O my soul!

O Lord, haste the day when the faith shall be sight,
The clouds be rolled back as a scroll;
The trump shall resound and the Lord shall descend;
Even so—it is well with my soul.

Truly, the release Mr. and Mrs. Spafford had to make in 1873 has not been wasted throughout the generations. The message of this great hymn of the Church has been a wellspring of hope and a proclamation of faith for countless people.

There's another kind of release that some mothers have to make in this season of their mothering journey. That's the release of an adult child into a lifestyle that goes cross-grain with almost everything they have been taught in their growing-up years.

This is an especially difficult release for a mother to make. To make a 20-year investment into a life and then have that investment literally seem for nothing almost goes beyond what the human heart can contain. The wounded mother's heart needs healing, and yet healing seems to evade the grasp unless she releases the child into the hands of God. This release, just like all the others, lets go of the child while holding tightly to God.

The wounded mother's heart needs healing,
and yet healing seems to evade the grasp unless
she releases the child into the hands of God.

One young man's dying words to his brother were, "Tell my story wherever it may help someone." To tell his story, of course, is to tell his mother's story. I tell her story, as well as his, with permission here as well.

She gave birth to three beautiful children, two boys and a girl. The baby girl died at birth, but the boys were strong and healthy. It was difficult to lose the life of her firstborn baby daughter; but she, like so many brave mothers before her, made a choice to focus on the blessing of life in the two children that remained. She never forgot her precious baby daughter, but focused on the stewardship of the lives that had been placed in her hands.

She had come to know the Lord in a personal way, even though her husband had not, and she was determined that her sons would enjoy the blessings of the Christian life. She was faithful to attend church and was actively involved in children's ministries all the years her sons were growing up. They shared the joy and fun of having a common bond in Christ.

When it came time, the oldest son went to Bible College and then became a pastor. What he had seen in his mother's life in the way of values and her relationship with the Lord had influenced him in his desires for the ministry.

During this time, the younger son began to seek out friendship from others. His father was an excellent provider for the family but wasn't around enough to develop a close emotional tie with either of his sons. This young man longed for male companionship. His loneliness seemed to haunt his every step. When it came time to go to college, he made the decision to go to a Christian College in hope of finding true friendship.

His brother introduced him to a minister friend, not knowing of the minister's sexual weaknesses. As they developed a friendship, the minister began to sexually molest the young man. When he attempted to get help from the school leaders, they threatened to dismiss him from school rather than understand his confusion and need for counsel. He withdrew from school and began to attend another church in town with the hope of getting help. Rather than getting the kind of help he desperately needed, he was molested by a person in that church as well. At this point, he not only withdrew from school and church, but from life as he knew it. The inner workings of his heart and thoughts became hidden from all those who knew and loved him.

Although his mother didn't understand all that was going through her son's mind, she released him to walk the pathway of his adult choices but held closely to him through prayer.

During those young adult years, he walked away from God and the family. He started a business that began to thrive. Seeming prosperity was all around him. He had new friends, a nice car and a flourishing business. *What more could he want out of life?*

His mother continued to pray for him and reach out to him as much as he would allow. He didn't have much time for her in those days; he invested himself in a friend that he felt understood him and his emotional needs more. Although his mother didn't understand their relationship, it didn't daunt her love for her son. She even invited his friend to family dinners and fellowship times. She was willing to take in another son, if only this son of her womb would return to the family bond.

Then his business began to go down financially. It continued to slide into financial debt until he could no longer hide it from her. At his request, she jumped in with sleeves rolled up and literally almost rescued the business through working and investing a lot of money into it. To her the money was a small price to pay, *for the prodigal son had returned.* Her heart was rejoicing once again.

His commitment to the business was short-lived. He walked away from it, leaving the once-again failing business at her doorstep. At the same time, his relationship with his friend ended. As a result of all these things, he asked if he could move back home. He went into a deep depression and spent days at a time in bed. His mother would talk to him and encourage him. *There was still so much more of life yet to be lived.* She prayed for him, served him and loved him in any way that she could.

One day he could no longer endure the loneliness and desperation that filled his heart. He decided to leave the safety of his home once again and return to his friends who walked a different pathway. Once again this mother released him while simultaneously holding on to him in prayer.

Once again this mother released him while simultaneously holding on to him in prayer.

He hadn't felt well in a while and so he got a physical checkup. The doctor's words came like a knife to his soul; "You are HIV-positive." When he later realized that he had full-blown AIDS and could no longer live on his own, once again he came back to the safety of his mother's arms of unconditional love. This time he came not with a need for an earthly rescue but with desperation in his heart to return to the God of his childhood. He came humbly, acknowledging that he had made many poor choices in life that had led him down a pathway of death and destruction.

The latter part of his days were more wonderful than any of his prior adult years, as he was restored to his natural family, his church family, and to his heavenly Father. Though the physical battle raged, communion was precious and sweet. His mother was there by his bedside day in and day out. She loved him, prayed for him, stood by him and released him into his final destiny. One day they'll meet again, on the "other side."

---

*She loved him, prayed for him, stood by him
and released him into his final destiny.*

How could her son's life be remembered, even though he died? Through his father, who made a decision to follow and serve the Lord so that he might see his son again in heaven. His life also lived on through his mother and his brother, who would embrace the message of his life and do as he requested— "tell his story wherever it may help someone."

---

*All mothers will experience releasing their children
into their ultimate destiny.*

Many mothers have experienced the death or the open rebellion of a child in some way; many have not. However, all mothers will experience releasing their children into their ultimate destiny. Regardless of whether it is a release to death or a release to marriage and career opportunities, it is a separation. Just as with the other releases in the journey of motherhood, once it takes place, life will never be the same. The experience may be hidden or it may be public, but it will be life-changing and powerful.

There is hidden influence in releasing your children. If you release them, they usually come back to you in joy. If you do not, they will pull away from you, causing pain to both of you. If you release them to walk out their own personal exciting adventure in God, their personal destiny, they will honor you. If you cling to them in desperation, they will either pull away or be stunted in their personal development by being under your shadow for too long. The options are clear, the choice is yours.

Life refuses to remain static; it demands progressive faith, and children do as well. Release your adult children to walk their walk and you will see reflected in their hearts and in their eyes the hidden power of a mother's heart.

Release your adult children to walk their walk and you will see reflected in their hearts and in their eyes the hidden power of a mother's heart.

Releasing is not easy, especially when you have worked hard at developing close friendships with your adult children. It is much easier to write about, talk about, and teach about than it is to do.

The fatal flaw of Christianity is love. I say "fatal" because true Christian love is unselfish and sacrificial, causing pain and joy simultaneously. This love will cause you to lay your life down for those you love. It believes the best, of others and of God and His destiny and plan for everyone concerned, including yourself. This love releases even when it hurts to the very core of your being.

My son and daughter-in-law were gone for two years serving the Lord on the other side of the nation. By the time the second year of their departure rolled around, I was "done," and wanted to pull them back home. I did not do what my heart yearned for. In fact, I did not even hint to them of my desire. Rather, I let them remain in the very hands of God, and today we have been blessed by their return to our side of the nation.

However, now our daughter and son-in-law and family have gone to the other side of the world to Cambodia, in the will of God. Once again, the colliding emotions that accompany releasing an adult child into their destiny are at war within my soul. One moment I am rejoicing in the goodness of God, and in the next, I am a puddle of despair on the floor of my prayer closet. The depth of these emotions have surprised me, as I have raised both of my children to have a world vision, so why should my soul be surprised by their walking this out? Why should it be "disquieted within me," as the Psalmist says?

My daughter and I are honest with each other; we have committed ourselves to being honest, all-the-while embracing the very heart and will of God. We cry and 'move on,' sometimes in strength and sometimes in weakness, but always in faith. My heart aches to see her face to face, not through a web cam, but eye-to-eye, heart-to-heart. My heart yearns to hear every inflection of her voice, which so easily enables me to read her heart, not through a phone line or an e-mail message or chat room, but voice-to-voice, whisper-to whisper, and chuckle-to chuckle.

We cry and 'move on,' sometimes in strength and sometimes in weakness, but always in faith.

As the years go by, I'll have my 'moments' I'm sure; but for now, I have my days and weeks. That's how grief and joy work together, one heals the other as they release each other to just "be." That's how releasing in love works, like a hand fitting into a well-worn glove, each embracing the other. Tears reflect both the joy and sorrow of the soul, what beauty they reflect on a countenance that trusts in God.

Life is what you have, not what you wished you had. Release comes to the journey of every mother. If you embrace the Heavenly Father as you release your child, your sorrows and your joys will be held safely in His reciprocal embrace. They will mean something to Him. He knows the fine lines and melodies of your heart; He created it to be tender to the touch and strong before the winds of adversity. He alone holds it ever so gently in His hands.

Life is what you have, not what you wished you had.

Even in the midst of this final release in motherhood, the confession of your heart must be, 'it truly is well with my soul.' That's what a genuine release costs—moments of joy and a peace that surpasses your understanding, and moments of tear-stained cheeks and a heart that aches so much that the body can feel it. The cost, however, never outweighs the benefits. Though we may not see the benefits this side of heaven, the Lord rewards those who trust in Him and give their very best into His care.

Most biblical scholars agree that Jesus made seven major statements on the Cross in the midst of excruciating physical, emotional, and spiritual pain and anguish. The third statement he made was directed to his mother and his beloved disciple John, recorded in John 19:26. When Jesus saw His mother there, and the disciple John standing nearby, he said to his mother, "Dear woman, here is your son," and to the disciple, "Here is your mother." From that time on, John took her into his home, as any son would.

Even when he was bearing the sin of the world, Jesus was concerned about his mother's welfare. Evidently, his younger brothers were too young to take full responsibility for their mother, and he felt the need to make sure she was well cared for.

His statement to John and her revealed that part of his purpose in dying was to bring a healing grace to families. He wanted to let the world know then and for all eternity that family relationships matter in redemption.

He wanted to let the world know then and for all eternity
that family relationships matter in redemption.

The further fruit of this is found in the fact that she, along with the other women and disciples went to the Upper Room and waited just as he instructed them to do. It is here in the Upper Room that we see Mary for the last time, waiting for her beloved son and the Holy Spirit he promised to send. It is here in the midst of his friends that she found herself bonded in fellowship.

As you've pondered the positive example of Mary's responses and releases in her motherhood journey, I pray that you've received a clear message that the only way to receive the grace to follow her example is through Jesus Christ, God's Son. When all is said and done, the greatest gift that you as a mother can receive from the life of Mary is not actually from her but from her son Jesus.

I hope you have enjoyed following her life and the lives of the other contemporary women found in these pages. Please know that I continue to pray for you in the same spirit the apostle Paul expressed:

I thank my God every time I remember you. In all my prayers for all of you, I always pray with joy because of your partnership in the gospel from the first day until now, being confident of this, that he who began a good work in you will carry it on to completion until the day of Christ Jesus. It is right for me to feel this way about all of you, since I have you in my heart. (Phil. 1:3-7)

Enjoy the journey, dear mother; you are in a worldwide fellowship of women who bear similar scars and joys deep within their hearts. Only you can affect your child in a way that 'only a mother can,' for you have within you The Hidden Power of a Mother's Heart.

Christ, Your Hope & Salvation

Apart from Christ we all live in Sin

PSALMS 51:5: *"Behold, I was brought forth in iniquity, and in sin my mother conceived me." (NASB)*

ROMANS 5:12-14: *"Therefore, just as through one man sin entered into the world, and death through sin, and so death spread to all men, because all sinned—for until the Law sin was in the world, but sin is not imputed when there is no law. Nevertheless death reigned from Adam until Moses, even over those who had not sinned in the likeness of the offense of Adam, who is a type of Him who was to come." (NASB)*

ISAIAH 64:6: *"For all of us have become like one who is unclean, and all our righteous deeds are like a filthy garment; and all of us wither like a leaf, and our iniquities, like the wind, take us away." (NASB)*

ROMANS 3:23: *"For all have sinned and fall short of the glory of God." (NASB)*

In Jesus Christ we all have the Hope of Salvation

ROMANS 5:19-21: *"For as through the one man's disobedience the many were made sinners, even so through the obedience of the One the many will be made righteous. The Law came in so that the transgression would increase; but where sin increased, grace abounded all the more, so that, as sin reigned in death, even so grace would reign through righteousness to eternal life through Jesus Christ our Lord." (NASB)*

ROMANS 3:21-26: *"But now apart from the Law the righteousness of God has been manifested, being witnessed by the Law and the Prophets, even the righteousness of God through faith in Jesus Christ for all those who believe; for there is no distinction; for all have sinned and fall short of the glory of Gid, being justified as a gift by His grace through the redemption which is in Christ Jesus whom God displayed publicly as a propitiation in His blood through faith. This was to demonstrate His righteousness, because in the forbearance of God He passed over the sins previously committed; for the demonstration, I say of His righteousness at the present time, so that He would be just and the justifier of the one who has faith in Jesus." (NASB)*

ISAIAH 53:6: *"All of us like sheep have gone astray, each of us has turned to his own way; but the Lord has caused the iniquity of us all to fall on Him." (NASB)*

Coming to Know Christ

Through Repentance

I JOHN 1:9: *"If we confess our sins, He is faithful and righteous to forgive us our sins and to cleanse us from all unrighteousness. If we say that we have not sinned, we make Him a liar and His word is not in us." (NASB)*

LUKE 5:31-32: *"And Jesus answered and said to them, 'It is not those who are well who need a physician, but those who are sick. I have not come to call the righteous but sinners to repentance.'" (NASB)*

2 CORINTHIANS 7:10: *"For the sorrow that is according to the will of God produces a repentance without regret, leading to salvation, but the sorrow of the world produces death." (NASB)*

ISAIAH 55:6-7: *"Seek the Lord while He may be found; call upon Him while He is near. Let the wicked forsake his way and the unrighteous man his thoughts; and let him return to the Lord, and He will have compassion on him, and to our God for He will abundantly pardon." (NASB)*

Through Faith—Believe

ROMANS 10:9-13: *"That if you confess with your mouth Jesus as Lord, and believe in your heart that God raised Him from the dead, you will be saved; for with the heart a person believes, resulting in righteousness, and with the mouth he confesses, resulting in salvation. For the Scripture says, 'Whoever believes in Him will not be disappointed.' For there is no distinction between Jew and Greek; for the same Lord is Lord of all, abounding in riches for all who call on Him; for 'Whoever will call on the name of the Lord will be saved.'" (NASB)*

JOHN 1:12: *"But as many as received Him, to them He gave the right to become children of God, even to those who believe in His name." (NASB)*

JOHN 3:14-18: *"As Moses lifted up the serpent in the wilderness even so must the Son of Man be lifted up; so that whoever believes will in Him have eternal life. For God so loved the world, that He gave His only begotten Son, that whoever believes in Him shall not perish, but have eternal life. For God did not send the Son into the world to judge the world, but that the world might be saved through Him. He who believes in Him is not judged; he who does not believe has been judged already, because he has not believed in the name of the only begotten Son of God." (NASB)*

I TIMOTHY 2:5-6: *"For there is one God, and one mediator also between God and men, the man Christ Jesus, who gave Himself as a ransom for all, the testimony given at the proper time." (NASB)*

Benefits of Salvation

ROMANS 5:1: *"Therefore, having been justified by faith, we have peace with God through our Lord Jesus Christ". (NASB)*

ROMANS 8:1,2: *"Therefore there is now no condemnation for those who are in Christ Jesus. For the law of the Spirit of life in Christ Jesus has set you free from the law of sin and of death." (NASB)*

ROMANS 6:23: *"For the wages of sin is death, but the free gift of God is eternal life in Christ Jesus our Lord." (NASB)*

NOTES

1   Isaiah 53:3-7 NIV

2   Palms 42:3-5 NIV

3   Delores Kuenning, *Helping People Through Grief,* (Minneapolis, Minnesota 55438, Bethany House Publishers, 1987), p. 15.

4   See Phil. 4:7

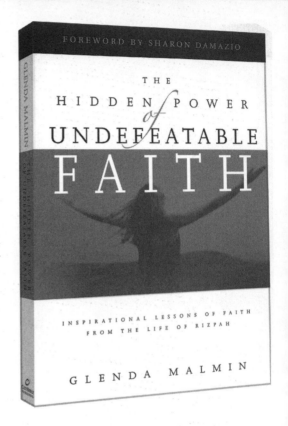

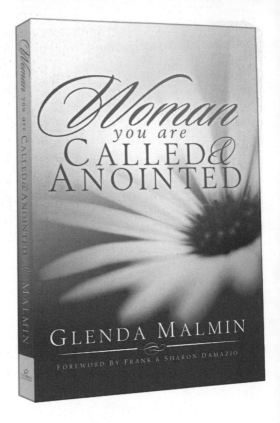

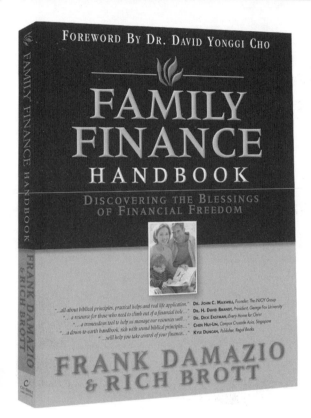

FAMILY FINANCE HANDBOOK

Discovering the Blessings of Financial Freedom

Frank Damazio & Rich Brott

With insights gained from twenty-five years in business and ministry, the authors impart to the reader biblical principles of stewardship and financial management. Readers learn how to get out of debt and are carefully guided through the investment process in this comprehensive and well-crafted resource. *Endorsed by Dr. John C. Maxwell, Dr. David Yonggi Cho, Dr. Dick Eastman, Dr. Phil Pringle, and others.*

Family Life / Finance / Christian Living

Softcover, 288 pages, 7 ½" X 10"
0-914936-60-3

GREAT FAITH

Making God Big

Wendell Smith

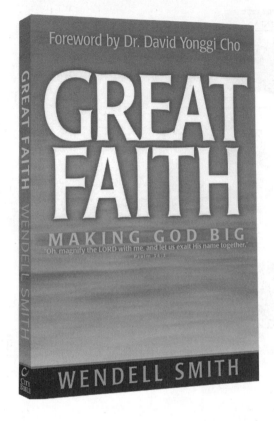

Wendell Smith's 30-year experience in ministry and pioneering a church in the Seattle area is the backdrop for his portrait of faith in the believer's life. His life demonstrates a balanced faith message that relates the Biblical concept of faith through a mixture of teaching and exhortation. This book will encourage Christians that faith can have a prominent role in their everyday lives. *Endorsed by Dr. David Yonggi Cho, Dr. Oral Roberts, Tommy Tenney, Marilyn Hickey, and others.*

Christian Living / Church Growth / Teachings of Christ

Softcover, 190 pages, 6" X 9"
1-886849-79-X

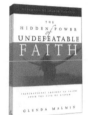

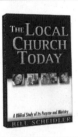
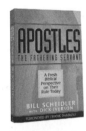

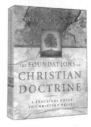

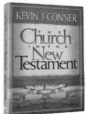